STYLE & PERSUASION

A Handbook
for Lawyers

NELSON JOHNSON, JSC (Ret.)

Other Books by Nelson Johnson

Boardwalk Empire:
The Birth, High Times and Corruption of Atlantic City

The Northside:
African Americans and the Creation of Atlantic City

Battleground New Jersey:
Vanderbilt, Hague and Their Fight for Justice

Darrow's Nightmare:
The Forgotten Story of America's Most Famous Trial Lawyer

THE NEW JERSEY INSTITUTE FOR CONTINUING LEGAL EDUCATION

The New Jersey Institute for Continuing Legal Education, a division of the New Jersey State Bar Association, has served the needs of the New Jersey bench and bar since 1962. From seminars and legal manuals to CLE On-Demand videos and other educational tools, our products are designed to provide the latest strategies, expert advice, and guidance to practitioners at every stage in their careers.

Our success in providing the legal community with the highest quality educational products would not be possible without the countless attorneys, doctors, dignitaries, and other legal experts who volunteer their efforts to serve as lecturers and authors. NJICLE is proud to be the conduit through which they share their knowledge, skills, and expertise with their fellow professionals. For more information about NJICLE seminars and publications, please visit NJICLE.com.

The material contained in this publication is for educational purposes only and is not intended to serve as a substitute for the professional services an attorney would normally provide to a client, including up-to-the-minute legal research.

Cover design by Alexia Garaventa

ISBN: 979-8-218-18842-9

Published in 2023 by the New Jersey State Bar Association

To: Hon. Steven P. Perskie, JSC (Ret.),
my longtime friend, ally,
mentor, critic, and editor of my writings

and

To: Sheryl McGrotty, my aide-de-camp of many years,
and the proofreader of all my writings

Acknowledgments

Writing about writing is something I've wanted to do for a long time. When I left the bench, I decided to consolidate my thoughts on writing that I had created over the years. Upon reviewing my files, I realized that I had prepared an outline for a writing handbook as early as 1982.

Not long after the release of my third book, *Battleground New Jersey*, which recounts the "political dirt" preceding the adoption of New Jersey's present-day constitution, I made the acquaintance of Lisa Spiegel, Esq., Director of the NJ Bar Association's ICLE program. Lisa introduced me to Dr. Robert Spangler, head of the NJSBA's Office on Marketing & IT. Discussions ensued and the idea for this handbook was hatched. Lisa and Bob have been supportive of all my efforts, and I have found their suggestions invaluable. I am grateful to call them friends.

Another person associated with the NJSBA is the editor, Cheryl Baisden. Cheryl's wisdom on word usage comes from her career in the newspaper business. At times, we struggled to get to the same place, but we always got there. Audio video manager Brian Altamura provided valuable criticism on the filming of the ten videos summarizing our handbook, creating our "vook." Finally, there is Brian Skulnik and Alexia Garaventa who led the way on the production and design of our handbook. The two of them provided valuable suggestions. At the end of the day, everyone's efforts were consistent with the ethos of the NJSBA, namely, the pursuit of excellence.

Discussion of Honoré Daumier Images

The five images of the sketches of the French Artist, Honoré Daumier (1808–1879) before each "Part" are in the public domain, online at Wikimedia Commons. These images were chosen for three reasons: **(1)** Your author's high school art history teacher knew he wanted to become an attorney and introduced him to an artist who began his career while working as a clerk in the French courts. **(2)** While still in his thirties, and fascinated by the work of attorneys, Daumier began drawing caricatures—"Les Gens de Justice"—depicting members of the legal profession. **(3)** Daumier always knew where he was going before he began his sketches. How do we know that? Years ago, while visiting the "Musee d'Orsay" in Paris, your author found not only original sketches made by Daumier but also dozens of individual clay busts. Those busts captured the images of all the people frequently appearing in his artwork. By doing the hard work of distilling the essence of his characters, and sculpting the details of their face and head in clay, Daumier was ready to go to work. In all your writings you must distill the facts, master the pertinent law, and create a "lead" before launching a serious discussion on any issue of importance to your client.

Table of Contents

Preface

"Easy reading means hard writing."
—William Thackeray

Why must you always communicate effectively? Because your success as an attorney depends on always being understood, regardless of your audience. Moreover, people you may never meet can form an opinion of you based on a single document you have written. You want your readers to respect you. To gain respect, you must first be understood. To get there, your words and thoughts must align. Yet, an effective writing style is about more than the reputation of an attorney; it is essential to the art of persuasion.

Three traits typify effective writers: **First,** the ability to distinguish between those words and structure that enhance your message versus those that impede it; **Second,** the ability to deploy syntax, diction, and rhythm to ensure your message flows, is understood, and is memorable; **Third,** the ability to craft sentences that engage your readers, prompting them to ponder your message. Your goal is simple, unadorned prose; writing that is lean, strong, and free of embellishment. None of that comes effortlessly. Yet, the more effort invested in your writing, the less effort required of your reader.

This book comprises ten chapters, plus Part Five, "A Thumbnail Sketch for the Busy Lawyer," which is a digested rendition of the ten chapters. Each chapter contains descriptive subtitles. I hope you will read this book in its entirety, but feel free to cherry-pick the subtitles. When you do, I'm confident you will find suggestions that will improve your writing style.

Nelson Johnson, JSC (Ret.)

MAKING SENSE OF THE NONSENSICAL

Aside from those engaged purely in literary pursuits, lawyers probably do more writing than any other professional...

—Judge Benjamin N. Cardozo

Lawyers are professional writers. We spend as much time putting our thoughts into words as do journalists, novelists and poets. Yet we face special problems. "[W]e have a history of wretched writing, a history that reinforces itself every time we open the lawbooks."[1] A large portion of our job entails squeezing knowledge from law books and guiding our clients through a thicket of court decisions, legislation and regulations—none of which speak to ordinary people. At times, our role is equivalent to an interpreter of foreign languages. We must make sense of nonsensical language from on high. Because the law is forever evolving, we are constantly learning new languages we must interpret for our clients.

Yet, frequently, *unlearning* something is harder than learning something new. My goal is to help you learn how to communicate effectively in every situation, whether it be with clients, colleagues, or the courts. Your goal should be writing that is direct, simple, brief, strong and lucid.

One of the strongest forces in the universe is inertia, and unless you commit to improving your methods of communicating, your writing will continue to rely upon much of the gibberish you learned in law school. Most of what we learned there, and much thereafter, was through reading the opinions of judges, then attempting to emulate their wisdom. Unfortunately, that emulation comes at a price—prose that can be very dense. Other writers don't suffer from such a handicap in the early years of their profession. As part of developing their writing style, journalists read well-constructed essays, novelists read classic works of literature and poets read great poetry, all providing valuable examples for writing well. Not so for lawyers. In our formative years, we read case law.

Unfortunately, few judicial decisions are inspiring. From my perspective, some of the most obtuse, footnote-laden, god-awful writing can be found in law journal essays and judicial opinions. Many scholarly writings by law school professors and judges are indeed brimming with wisdom, akin to veins of gold waiting to be mined. But most of these authors seem indifferent to the fact that extracting wisdom from their knowledge would be much easier had it been presented in an engaging style.

Indeed, style matters. Take a moment to read aloud an appellate court ruling or a law review article to a friend or family member. You will likely laugh or cry by the end of the second page. Generally, the only people who read these learned primers are other judges, legal scholars and affected lawyers. For many judges and legal scholars, these writings are rarely about simplifying an issue, they are about expounding on the law, layer upon layer. The more intricate and complex their discussion, including an abundance of footnotes, the better. Though reading such works is unavoidable, mimicking their writing style guarantees you will never be an effective communicator. Few lawyers have such a captive audience. We must communicate not only with courts and our colleagues but, more importantly, with the people who pay our fees, namely clients.

Examine your daily routine and you will see that a large part of your role as an attorney is that of a professional writer, explaining the law to others. With the exception of lawyers on their feet daily in a courtroom, every other attorney conveys most information in written form. As a result, you must think like a professional writer. Clarity, in everything you write and say, must be your primary concern. Your writing must effortlessly impact your readers' thinking or you have failed.

In my years on the bench, I presided over hundreds of jury trials. Before each trial, I reminded the lawyers, "It's not the jury's job to figure out your presentation, it's your job to make yourself understood." That is true of every communication you make as an attorney, whether written or spoken. The more effort invested in your writing, the less required of your reader.

We all have audiences to whom we wish to deliver information. In our profession, we never know with certainty who our audience is. An email, letter, contract, memorandum or brief on a motion may be read by many sets of eyes before its message is delivered to every interested party. As a professional writer in the law, the words used to express your thoughts on any matter must not be misunderstood. Readers must readily grasp your meaning or you have missed the mark.

To avoid frustration with your writing, be mindful of four terms that course through this book: the first three are *precise, concise and economy of language.* In all your writing, you must strive to be precise and concise, and to use as few words—and syllables—as appropriate for the topic and your audience. Increasing the word count rarely conveys a thought more clearly, but the right choice of words always does. The fourth term I have used in presentations to lay audiences on the craft of writing is *the reader's eye.* Just as a speaker must be sensitive to the ears of his audience, so as not to bore or confuse, writers must be ever mindful of how their prose will be received by the reader's eye. There must be nothing in your writing that creates an obstacle to your reader's eye moving effortlessly across the page, sentence by sentence, paragraph by paragraph.

From time to time, I will refer to "Strunk & White." William Strunk Jr. and E.B. White were the authors of *The Elements of Style*, a renowned handbook on writing. This authoritative manual is in its fourth edition and retains relevance for all writers, including lawyers.

Finally, I have a confession. I own *many* books on writing; I've read approximately half in their entirety. As for the remainder, I scanned the table of contents and index to read those portions that interested me most. My hunch is many readers of this handbook will do the same. Thus, what follows is a string of words and phrases that appear multiple times in this handbook to capture the eye of the busy lawyer. Don't be surprised when you see them repeated, and keep these concepts at the forefront of your thinking: less is more; simple unadorned prose; economy of language; the reader's eye; the more effort you put into your writing, the less effort required of your reader; words matter; simple declaratory sentences; matter of factly; sentences are like fences; mastery of the facts; know your deal; you win your case by making your case; it's all about your sentences;

understand your client's needs, situations and expectations; clarity; cogency; lucidity; brevity demonstrates confidence; you must prepare an outline; there is no excuse for footnotes; and writing is rewriting.

Part One

UNLEARNING BAD HABITS

*I think that law should be a literary profession,
and the best legal practitioners regard law
as an art as well as a craft.*

—Justice Ruth Bader Ginsberg

Chapter One

LESS IS MORE

Contents

1.1 The Reader's Eye

Following the publication of my first book, I was asked to speak at several writing conferences. The first event was thrilling yet daunting. In preparing my notes for the first conference, I was struggling with how best to explain the concept of "linking." I wanted my audience to understand more than how the use of strong nouns, verbs or modifiers in the last sentence of one paragraph, then re-appearing in the first sentence of the next paragraph, will "link' the two paragraphs. I needed to show, not tell. That's when I decided to express my personal aim as a writer. My number one goal is for the "reader's eye" to glide effortlessly across my writing, sentence by sentence, paragraph by paragraph, page by page. Especially as attorneys, we must make things easy for our readers. We are interpreting the law for people with a need to know. We mustn't litter our readers' path with unnecessary lawyerly words and long-winded phrases and sentences. Nothing should hinder the reader's eye as it makes its journey through your prose.

Reading requires more of the reader than we sometimes appreciate. Each sentence, paragraph and page conveys thoughts that must be digested. That mental digestive process demands of the reader that she make use of her reasoning powers by defining, classifying and making logical inferences. The simpler the words, the shorter the sentences and the more engaging the construction of the text, the smoother the journey for the reader's eye. Your choice of words, length of sentences and paragraphs, along with your syntax, diction and rhythm, must all be calculated to encourage the reader's eye to glide across the page.

Words matter. If you wish to capture your reader's attention, you must make it your practice to treat words with respect. Any word that impedes the reader's eye must be omitted or replaced. You must develop the habit of scrutinizing everything you write; needless words must be deleted. All good writing is the product of rewriting. It's unusual that the first draft of any substantial presentation will be of the quality you desire, namely, simple unadorned prose that impacts your reader. As discussed in Chapter Seven, with practice, patience and persistence, editing your own work will come naturally.

Equally important as some of the skill sets discussed in this handbook is the "context" in which we work as professional writers. It is frequently said: "People's attention spans have shrunk." I see things differently. We live in the most highly commercialized society in the history of civilization. Add the Internet and social media, and it's a mix that troubles psychologists, sociologists and educators. From the moment we awake until we go to bed, whether driving in our car, surfing the web, opening mail (electronic and snail), watching television or looking at our cellphone, we are constantly bombarded with messages of one sort or another. Advertising resources seem infinite.

Yet human attention is one of the more finite resources. To describe the demand for human attention, one social psychologist uses the term "the attention economy." Advertising is part of the attention economy; so are sports, politics, religion, journalism, all forms of entertainment, literature, social media platforms and, alas, even lawyers' communications. It's the nature of things that when you pay attention to one thing, you ignore everything else. "In an attention economy, *one is never not on*, at least when one is awake, since one is nearly *always paying, getting or seeking* attention."[1] (emphasis added) The average person's attention span hasn't withered; it's overwhelmed. Understanding that distinction is critical to your ability to communicate effectively.

Your success as a communicator depends upon your ability to penetrate the mind and gain the interest of an audience being barraged with messages. Not an easy task. Your message must be tailored to swim in that rushing river of information. To grab your reader's attention, your writing must stand out in a way that pleases the reader's eye. All your research and carefully conceived positions run the risk of being ignored if you fail to structure your thoughts in a manner readily accessible by the reader. Don't litter your writing with "legaldegook."[2]

1.2 The Other Gettysburg Address

Attorneys are some of the most verbose people in our society. Whether trying to impress clients, colleagues or judges with their knowledge, or battling the fear of failing to address every conceivable issue, lawyers tend to say too much. While my primary focus is writing, many of the rules of restraint on writing apply with equal force to the spoken word. Less is more. The fewer words used to express your thoughts, the greater the likelihood they will be understood, remembered and embraced. Economy equals impact. A thimble full of simple words is a weapon, while a bucket full of highfalutin nonsense may doom you with your reader. Too many words tend to turn your message into mush. There is power in brevity.

For proof of brevity's power to inform as well as its capacity to linger in the mind, we can look to Gettysburg, Pennsylvania, on November 19, 1863. That day, at the dedication of the national cemetery on the site where more than 3,000 soldiers died and 15,000 were wounded, the featured speaker was Edward Everett, America's most sought-after speaker. Everett was a distinguished historian who had served as president of Harvard, U.S. congressman, governor of Massachusetts, secretary of state and U.S. senator. Remembrance of the dead was the theme of his oration. Everett used ancient Greece and its battle with the Persians to make sense of the carnage at Gettysburg. His remarks consumed nearly two *hours*. Everett was followed by President Abraham Lincoln.

Lincoln had little of Everett's education. He had studied history, science and math on his own but read neither Greek nor Latin. Recalling his youth in frontier Illinois, he once wrote, "If a straggler supposed to understand Latin, happened to sojourn in the neighborhood, he was looked upon as a wizard." Following Everett, the president spoke for approximately two *minutes*. Lincoln's speech totaled 272 words; 74 percent were single syllables. As for the polysyllabic words and phrases, most packed a wallop, such as, *consecrate, hallow, struggled, dedicated to the proposition, thus far so nobly advanced,* and *shall not perish from the earth.* Multiple words frequently repeated; his speech comprised a paltry 130 unique words. Lincoln addressed profound issues with simplicity, and the use of ordinary language elevated rather than diminished his message. The Gettysburg Address will remain one of the best-remembered and most-quoted speeches for as long as our nation exists. The next day, Everett wrote to Lincoln: "I should be glad, if I could flatter myself that I came as near to the central idea of the occasion, in two hours, as you did in two minutes."

None of us will attain Lincoln's mastery of language, but that doesn't mean we can't learn from his example, striving for simplicity in all our communications. A rule of thumb you would do well to embrace in drafting letters, briefs and memoranda, goes like this: when a four-syllable word works as well as a five-syllable word, use four; when three works as well as four, use three; when two works as well as three, use two; and when one works as well as two, use one. It may seem trite, but as you develop the habit of simplifying your choice of words, your writing will gain greater power to persuade. Once you get the knack of it, you will be stunned at the number of one-syllable words that can make your point. (*Note:* 20 of the 22 words in the preceding sentence are one syllable.) Finally, during the past two generations brevity has taken a beating. There's been a development in the legal community that tends to increase the length of lawyers' messages.

1.3 A Legal Brief Must Be "Brief"

Decades ago, early in my career, following an oral argument on a motion involving injunctive relief, my adversary and I had a conversation with the late Vincent Haneman, recently retired from the New Jersey Supreme Court. In the 1970s, in New Jersey, a retired Supreme Court Justice wishing to do "senior recall" could pretty much do so in any court he chose. On this occasion, Justice Haneman was sitting in the Atlantic County Chancery Court, hearing applications for temporary restraining orders. After one such hearing, he met with two young lawyers to discuss our briefs.

As best as I can recall Haneman gently spoke to us: "I could tell at a glance that your briefs were much too long for the issues raised by the dispute before the court. The length was a dead giveaway. If I had a law clerk of my own, I would have expected him to let me know if there was anything in your submissions worth reading. If not, I would have skimmed over your papers and relied upon my clerk's memorandum in preparing my questions for oral argument." Justice Haneman then remarked that at the trial level, except for summary judgment motions, legal briefs should never exceed 10–12 pages. As for dispositive motions and appeals, he was of the opinion that 20–25 pages were usually sufficient for making an argument.

In confirmation of Justice Haneman's thoughts on the length of legal briefs, when you consider that one double-spaced page contains 325–350 words, 25 pages yield in excess of 8,000 words. That's a generous word budget to make a legal argument. The typical chapter of a general nonfiction book rarely exceeds 7,000 words. Why, if properly organized, does a legal argument truly need to be more than 8,000 words? Yet that's not where we are today. Why? We need to look no further than the opinions written by judges at all levels.

1.4 Role Models Lured by Technology

It's hard to argue that judges are good role models when it comes to being precise and concise. In the past two generations, the length of judicial opinions has grown excessive. Yet in the pre-technology age, most judicial opinions exemplified economy of language. What happened? How did we go astray? Follow me.

In 1954, U.S. Supreme Court Chief Justice Earl Warren issued his memorable opinion in *Brown vs. Board of Education.*[3] Including footnotes, it contains fewer than 4,000 words. In *Brown,* the Supreme Court extended the "equal protection of the laws" guaranteed by the 14th Amendment to every student in our nation's public schools. The Court declared that the doctrine of "separate but equal" announced three generations earlier in *Plessy vs. Ferguson,* had no place in public schools. Prior to the adoption of civil rights legislation by Congress, Chief Justice Warren made it clear that regardless of state law, the "privileges or immunities of citizens of the United States" cannot be abridged. *Brown* remains a clarion call for the guarantee of equal rights of all citizens.

Now compare *Brown* with *District of Columbia vs. Heller.*[4] Written by Justice Antonin Scalia in 2008, *Heller* held that the Second Amendment guarantees an individual's right to possess firearms. The high court found that a local ordinance banning handguns and requiring firearms in the home to be kept nonfunctional was a violation of the petitioner's rights. Why did Justice Scalia need over 17,000 words to express himself on the Second Amendment? The answer is, he didn't need to use that many words; he did so because technology enabled him to do so.

Technology enables prolix prose. The ability to sit down before a computer screen and begin pecking away plays a large role in where we are today. Working from their handwritten notes, judges of earlier generations generally wrote their initial opinions in longhand, and some dictated them. Then, they made successive revisions of the document, edited and re-edited, typed and re-typed by a secretary, until the opinion was finalized. Thanks to information technology and user-friendly software and training in computer keyboards, it's the rare law clerk, attorney or judge who can't do much of the work themselves, especially revisions. In the *Heller* decision, Justice Scalia and his law clerks could go online to research court decisions and historical facts to support his ruling. They were then able to copy and paste from those online documents without the need for additional typing to insert new text into the working draft; and finally, they could make needed revisions without exhausting themselves. Advances in technology have produced a glut of words and spawned long-winded documents by judges and lawyers alike.

One example of wordy, ponderous prose enabled by technology is a paragraph from a 22-page, over 7,000 word ruling involving a running back with the Dallas Cowboys.

> Outside of limited circumstances, the failure to "fully exhaust" contracted for "grievance procedures" places an employee's claim for breach of a collective bargaining agreement beyond "judicial review." Vaca v. Sipes, 386 U.S. 171, 184–85 (1967) (discussing situations where an "employee may obtain judicial review of his breach-of-contract claim despite his failure to secure relief through the contractual remedial procedures"). While courts have jurisdiction to enforce collective bargaining contracts, "where the contract provides grievance and arbitration procedures, those procedures must first be exhausted and courts must order resort to the private settlement mechanisms without dealing

with the merits of the dispute." Misco, 484 U.S. at 37. Our circuit holds that federal courts lack subject matter jurisdiction "to decide cases alleging violations of a collective bargaining agreement ... by an employee against his employer unless the employee has exhausted contractual procedures for redress." Meredith v. La. Fed'n of Teachers, 209 F.3d 398, 402 (5th Cir. 2000).[5]

Wearisome to the reader's eye, this phrase is even worse on the ear. Try reading it aloud. Worse still, this 157-word paragraph is accompanied by a 93-word footnote (mercifully, not shown) at the bottom of the page, amplifying a sentence that began on the previous page. Reading the court's ruling is both tortuous and torturous.[6] How did our profession get to the point where these types of rulings are common? The computer is the culprit. So, what's the answer? Restraint, restraint and organization. As discussed in Chapter Three, a "word budget" can be helpful in shaping your thoughts. Learning to restrain the flow of words from your head to a computer screen is critical to getting your message across to your intended audience. Economy of language must be an attorney's priority. Our society suffers from a glut of words. We have to work at keeping things simple; if we don't, we can be crushed by the volume of information bombarding us. This works to a lawyer's advantage. You need only seize the moment.

Your advantage is that our profession is part of the service economy. Most people with whom you interact need your help in solving a problem involving the law. The more simply you can get your clients through their difficulties, the better. Given the assorted members of your potential audience, people interested in a particular legal issue—clients, colleagues, and judges— you are fortunate. Unlike salespeople, politicians, journalists, educators, etc., you don't have to fight for your audience's attention; generally, you already have it. Why? Clients are paying for your advice. Usually, they read whatever is submitted to them, provided they understand it. Your colleagues, whether friends or foes, have an interest in being informed of the position you are advancing on behalf of your clients. As for judges and decision-makers across all forums, they are held to high standards and can only act responsibly following an understanding of your submissions. So, you start with a captive audience. Your goal is to monopolize the attention of your ready-made audience by convincing them of the worth of your message.

1.5 The Length of Your Message Matters

Far too often lawyers write and speak as though quantity yields quality. Not so. It's the force of your message, not the number of words, that produces favorable results. You must have the confidence to be brief, namely, short and to the point. You must hone your message down to its essence. A writer's goal should always be to use "the fewest and shortest words that will cover one's meaning. What is above all needed, is to let the meaning choose the word not the other way around."[7] Your writing will be assessed based upon cogency, lucidity and the penetration of analysis. Pouring one word upon another does not win the day, clarity does.

One role model in clarity was my first mentor in the law, John Bertman. John was a University of Pennsylvania Wharton School and Law School graduate and was as frugal with his words as he was with his money in managing his law practice. Some of his letters to clients and attorneys were so short that his secretary teased him, calling them "JB cryptograms." It was rare that his letters went to a third page, and the majority were limited to one page, typically 200–350 words. As for his legal briefs, unless moving for, or defending against, a dispositive motion, they generally were little more than dozen pages, or less than 5,000 words. John's certifications, whether for a client or himself as counsel, were typically three pages or fewer. Contracts and agreements of any sort—everything from the sale of a business or a matrimonial settlement to an employment contract—usually were five to seven pages, with needed exhibits attached. The same held true for John's initial pleadings to commence litigation; complaints were ordinarily five to seven pages. During my first few years as an attorney, whenever I presented a document for John's review, it was returned with whole portions deleted. On occasion, John's methods bruised my ego but the message never suffered.

When asked about his method for beginning a letter, document or pleading, John often replied, "Before starting, always know your deal." John used the term "deal" figuratively for everything from responding to another lawyer's letter, drafting an agreement settling a business dispute, or preparing an emergent petition seeking injunctive relief. In order to "know your deal," a lawyer must understand his client's needs, situation and expectations. The lawyer must appreciate the context of the matter being handled. Finally, the lawyer must think through the details of the facts and the controlling law. Prior to beginning a draft of whatever I was writing, John advised that "Legal writing isn't free form, First, organize your thoughts." Some of his outlines were little more than scribblings on the back of the letter to which he was replying, but he knew what they meant. Once his outline was completed, John was ready to begin dictating his first draft. Admittedly, the legal world in which John began practicing law—1958—has been transformed. The

Internet and digital revolution have both simplified and complicated our lives.

Yet, this increased complication cries out for simplification. Clients don't pay you for the length of a legal brief or the number of cases cited, nor are judges impressed by these things. What captures the reader's attention is a straightforward discussion, using simple language, that explains the issues to be addressed. Though for clients it's the result that matters most; even clients unhappy with the outcome will usually be satisfied with the legal representation received if the lawyer has communicated with them effectively. A court, whether a judge or a jury, only wants to know if your arguments cogently address the issues at hand. Brevity demonstrates confidence and enhances credibility. In every instance, a lawyer's reward for her efforts is based upon the quality of the message, not the quantity of the words used to present it.

Chapter Two

DISCARDING LEGALISMS & NOMINALIZATIONS

Contents

2.1 You Win Your Case by Making Your Case

In nearly everything you write, a lawyer should start with the mindset that she has the burden of persuasion on the issues at hand. It need not be a formal adversarial proceeding, but simply a situation in which your client's position has been (or will be) challenged and you must advance a convincing argument. When you have the burden, the best means by which to *make your case* is by mastering the facts.

To a greater extent than is helpful for many attorneys, the discussion of judicial opinions in law school takes on too much importance, leaving the impression that facts are fungible. Some lawyers believe that finding the controlling case law is the be-all, end-all. Not so. Case law is generally supple and malleable. "Facts are stubborn things."[1] Facts can be dissected, shaded and framed but once fully known and conceded, can never be changed. Having a firm grasp of all relevant facts is where you must begin. Only then do you concern yourself with case law. Your grip upon the facts will empower you to briefly explain why your client's position meets the burden of persuasion. Thus, before you dive into the case law, you must distill your facts to their essence. Then you must be able to present those facts in simple declaratory statements using ordinary language.

Each of the summary statements below is of a nature that the facts supporting it could comprise hundreds of pages in pre-trial discovery, yet each is a single sentence of 25 words or less, free of legalisms. The statements are loosely based on pleadings filed years ago in connection with proceedings in the New Jersey Superior Court. In each instance, these facts were readily available prior to the filing of a lawsuit and ultimately proved decisive in resolving the dispute between the parties.

- Multiple potential wrongdoers were crowded into the barroom; my client was the only one who was sober and had no history with the victim.

- Defendant has violated the post-employment restrictive covenant; the only question is damages owed for the accounts stolen from his former employer.

- As documented by three senior employees, on multiple occasions, the supervisor ignored my client's complaints of harassment, culminating in a sexual assault.

- Defendant's over-the-counter medication was FDA approved 40 years ago and is only one of 7–8 drugs ingested by Plaintiff.

Boiled-down facts, reduced to the crux of the matter, are what every lawyer must strive to create as early as possible when retained to represent a client. Regardless of which party to an encounter you represent—the buyer of commercial property, an employee suing an employer, or an injured person versus a property owner—all share a common concern. Though some standards of the law will likely assign the legal *burden of proof* as to the parties' interactions, a lawyer communicating on behalf of his client always has *a burden to persuade* everyone involved as to the correctness of the client's position on the issues at hand. Regardless of the law's impact on your client, once you master the facts you are on a path toward a more favorable resolution of the matter.

You win your case by making your case. *You don't* make your case by delving into minutiae and overanalyzing the circumstances; *you don't* make your case with long-winded dissertations on the law, and *you especially do not* make your case by trashing the other side. You make your case by boiling down the available information to a handful of relevant words gleaned from the known facts that everyone can (indeed must) accept. There is no substitute for total command of the facts. Once you have written several simple declaratory statements (three to five sentences, 50–75 words) demonstrating that you have mastered the essential facts, your client's position will be substantially enhanced.

2.2 Discard Lawyerly Legalisms

Lawyers and their use of words are often the butt of jokes. As once quipped by Will Rogers, "The minute you read something that you can't understand, you can almost be sure that it was drawn up by a lawyer."[2] Being understood is your primary goal. Sound legal writing ought to be little more than mainstream English applied to the law. The lawyer whose writing is layered in jargon shouldn't delight in the mastery of such terms and phrases, but rather should purposefully set about to cast them aside. Too often, legal jargon consists not only of language from statutes, antiquated terms derived from Latin, and the inscrutable piffle in government regulations but also stilted words and phrases that undermine the strength of your message. Most archaic phrases have little to no substantive value. They just get in the way. Terms such as *witnesseth, arguendo, obiter dicta, de facto, in pari delicto, in loco parentis* and *prima facie* are tedious terms that we learned in law school listening to our professors and reading the opinions of dead judges.

Some of the hardest things to *unlearn* are the legalisms learned in law school. When you were a law student, you read and digested thousands of court opinions. It was inevitable that you would internalize aspects of that style of writing. Admittedly, it's a hard habit to break. But think about your first year in law school and ask yourself: "How easy was it for me to read those decisions for the first time? Why should non-lawyers readily absorb legalese when I struggled with it?"

With a struggle, law school taught us that in order to sound like a lawyer, there was a special jargon that students had to adopt. The allure of such terms lies in the quest to appear as someone who is learned in his profession, a notch above mere mortals untrained in the law. True, all professions have their own jargon. Everyone, from doctors, scientists, and engineers to accountants, educators, and police officers, uses dozens of terms and phrases unique to their training, many of them unintelligible to everyone else. Fortunately for them, their audience is generally limited to their peers. What's more, words are not as integral to their livelihood as they are for lawyers, who have the burden of persuasion. As professional writers, you rise and fall, prosper or don't, based upon the words you use. Modeling yourself after law school professors rarely makes for effective communications with non-lawyers. At the end of the day, the people who pay your fees don't want their problems explained in legaldegook.

It's critical to your success that you make every effort to abandon legalese in all your communications. Think of lawyerly legalisms as excess baggage; their presence requires the reader's eye to drag them along during its journey across the page. Always be mindful of the fact that before the reader's eye found its way to your prose, it first had to swim through a torrent of written communications, all part of the digital age. Upon arriving at your handiwork, the reader's eye may not have the stamina for wearisome legalisms and larded phrases, placing the effective delivery of your message in jeopardy.

Though legalisms play a large role in the things you read, you cannot permit them to pollute what you write. They will choke your message, surely as if someone had a hold on your throat. Unnecessary legalisms and burdensome phrases are sand in the reader's eye. Yet by being a bit creative in your writing and respecting every word you use, most legalisms can be readily translated into prose that is well-suited for the reader's mental digestive process. The brief list that follows will hopefully stimulate your thinking and help you appreciate the need to eliminate legalisms from your writing.

Legalisms	Mainstream English
acknowledge the applicability	note the relevance
adjoining	next to
adequate number of	sufficient
ad seriatim	point by point
as to	about, by, for
at the present time	now
by means of	by
contiguous to	next to
determine and effectuate	decide and complete
during such time as	while
endeavored to elucidate	tried to explain
for the duration of	during
in as much as	because
in lieu of	instead
in the event that	if
in the interest of	for
notwithstanding the fact that	although
previous to	before
sought to interpose	tried to insert
subsequent to	after
thereafter	later
the reason being that	because
unencumbered communication	free speech
until such time	until

This list is hardly exhaustive, and is intended merely to illustrate my point. Use your imagination. Often, avoiding legalisms is as simple as reflecting on the word count of what you want to say. If you examine the above columns, you will see that in every instance mainstream English is comprised of fewer syllables. Most lawyer-like terms and phrases can be readily translated into ordinary English. Ask yourself when you are about to use a phrase such as "notwithstanding the fact that," will fewer words suffice? *Although* works well. Think about that, one word consisting of two syllables versus four words comprised of seven syllables. Which is easier on the reader's eye? Because some phrases frequently appear in statutes, court rules and judicial decisions (e.g., *habeas corpus, ultra vires, res ipsa loquitur, ex post facto* and *res judicata*) it's impossible to entirely eliminate some terms from all your writings. Still, it's important that you routinely use plain language wherever possible.

Another example of the law having one foot in the past, clinging to legalisms, is the stringing together of common words to create phrases presented in a sing-song style. Though delivering little substance, legal doublets such as "null and void," "due and payable" or "final and conclusive," and legal triplets such as "grant, bargain and sell," "give, devise and bequeath" or "rest, residue, remainder" are throwbacks to a long-past era. They are holdovers from 12th–15th Century England, the era in which our common law began to evolve. The common law we know today dates back to the 12th and 13th centuries during the reign of King Henry II, who appointed judges to resolve disputes among his subjects. The meaning of the term *common law* was twofold. *First,* the English Court of Common Pleas handled disputes among *commoners;* and *second,* the mission of those courts was to create a collective body of law based upon local customs, that is, a unified system of law *common* throughout all of England.

When our common law was developing in the early English courts, it was necessary to translate old English into French (to satisfy the Normans) and, likewise, into Latin (to appease the Roman Catholic Church), to ensure there were no misunderstandings when preparing official documents, conducting legal proceedings or solemnizing church ceremonies. Though they persist, such translations are no longer necessary. Whether preparing an affidavit, pleading or contract, when bundles of two or three words all mean the same thing, one will do.

2.3 Nominalizations

Hand-in-hand with legalisms is the inclination toward nominalizations, unnecessarily turning verbs into nouns. One writing expert refers to this phenomenon as "creeping nounism,"[3] the tendency to prefer nouns over verbs. Another learned observer calls it "a new American disease."[4] One of my favorite ways to characterize this lurch into dim-witted writing is "the noun plague"[5] which issues death sentences to a writer's sentences with stupefying regularity.

Below are four examples of bad writing caused by nominalizations, with suggested revisions.

1. I do not dispute the correctness of his observation.

   I agree that what he observed is correct.

2. Pitiless retribution was administered with bureaucratic coldness and inflexibility.

   Revenge was dispensed by a cold and inflexible bureaucracy.

3. Perhaps in recognition of the weakness of its attempt to distinguish Miller, the Court argues in the alternative that Miller should be discounted because of its decisional history.[6]

   Perhaps the Court recognizes that its attempt to distinguish Miller is weak and instead argues that the decisions relied upon in Miller aren't sound precedent.

4. Female employees were responsible for deliverance of excellent customer service and the creation of a feeling of classiness and sensuality to build customer loyalty.

   In an effort to secure loyal customers, female employees needed to excel at creating a sensual feeling of class.

During the past 50 years, serious students of the English language have witnessed a plague that transformed verbs, and occasionally adjectives, into mind-numbing polysyllabic nouns. "Unnecessary abstraction is one of the worst faults of modern writing—the string of nouns held together by prepositions and relying on the passive voice convey the enfeebled sense."[7] Most observers believe nominalizations are an outgrowth of scholarly studies—first the sciences and engineering, then history and law—wherein the authors seek to demonstrate their objectivity by removing themselves entirely from the text. What they fail to appreciate is that it saps vitality from their message. The result is writing that "becomes flabby and obscure because the lack of agents and of strong verbs deprives the sentence of its due motive and power and needed signposts."[8] There are few things more tiresome to the reader's eye than several four- or five-syllable words preceded by a weak verb.

As defined by the Merriam-Webster Dictionary, nominalization is "the process or result of forming a noun or noun phrase from a clause or a verb." But what type of noun? One respected linguist has coined the term "zombie nouns" to characterize words that "cannibalize active verbs, suck the lifeblood from adjectives and substitute abstract entities for human beings." [9] The same linguist incisively illustrated her point:

> The proliferation of nominalizations in a discursive formation may be an indication of a tendency toward pomposity and abstraction.

> The sentence above contains no fewer than seven nominalizations, each formed from a verb or an adjective. Yet it fails to tell us who is doing what. When we eliminate or reanimate most of the zombie nouns (tendency becomes tend, abstraction becomes abstract) and add a human subject and some active verbs, the sentence springs back to life:

> Writers who overload their sentences with nominalizations tend to sound pompous and abstract. [10]

Bureaucrats, academics and economists seem to relish the opportunity to take a verb or adjective and transform it into a colorless noun. Whatever the cause of nominalization, we can add lawyers to the list of professionals whose writing has been infected. As professional writers you must make it your practice to eliminate nominalizations from your writing. For starters, these soulless creatures are often recognized by their endings, such as: __ance, __ation, __ency, __ian, __ion, __ism, __ity, ment or __ness.

For some reason, those writers who seem intent on writing in a "professional" or "academic" tone end up fixated on nouns. Instead of writing "I analyzed the data," they write, "A data analysis was performed." Instead of simply "Sarah explained," they opt for, "Sarah delivered an explanation." Beware of nominalizations. Verbs give life, color and action to your writing. When given an option between a verb and a noun—take the verb.

Verb	Nominalization
accuse	accusation
affirm	affirmation
allocate	allocation
argue	argument
behave	behavior
calculate	calculation
consider	consideration
describe	description
direct	direction
distort	distortion
evaluate	evaluation
involve	involvement
mediate	mediation
observe	observation
persist	persistence
plagiarize	plagiarism
recall	recollection
reveal	revelation
timely	timeliness
terminate	termination

Avoiding reference to human beings and their actions are the primary reason nominalizations yield bland, boring, mind-numbing writing. Effective writing employs actors and action. No one *does* anything in a sentence like: "Limitations on driving speeds are the creation of government." It is more precise and interesting to say, "Speed limits on driving were created by our legislators." To be certain that you have not fallen into this bad habit, check on the number of *-tion* and *-ance* words found in the first draft of your writings. The bigger the number, the more likely your writing has been infected by "the noun plague."

Contrast the wordy and vague nominalized phrase with the more precise revision:

Nominalized Phrase	Revision
gave a report	reported
made a decision	decided
offered a suggestion	suggested
issued an announcement	announced
served as a catalyst	catalyzed
made a measurement	measured
entered an order	ordered
resulted in an increase	increased
issued a proclamation	proclaimed
made an assertion	asserted
led to the destruction of	destroyed
resulted in failure	failed
made an observation	observed
granted deference to	deferred
made a recitation	recited

2.3.1 Identifying and Revising Nominalizations

1. **When the nominalization is the subject of an empty verb, change the nominalization to a verb and find a new subject.**

   It is the court's intention to review the lawyers' briefs by next Tuesday

   The court intends to review the lawyers' briefs by next Tuesday.

2. **When the nominalization follows an empty verb, change the nominalization to a verb that can replace the empty verb.**

   The attorney conducted an interrogation of the witness.

   The attorney interrogated the witness.

3. **When a nominalization follows a *there is/are/was*, change the nominalization to a verb and find a new subject.**

   There was widespread anger among lawyers at the Supreme Court ruling.

   Many lawyers were angered by the Supreme Court ruling.

4. **When you find two nominalizations close together, change the first into a verb. Then either leave the second as it is or turn it into a verb in a clause addressing *why* or *how*.**

   There was initially a consideration of the testimony of the witness by the judge.

   Initially, the judge considered the witness's testimony.

   Initially, the judge considered how (why) the witness testified.

Despite everything said above, an occasional zombie noun won't destroy your writing. Yet, you must be mindful of weak/ empty verbs followed by abstractions that are really just verbs transformed into awkward nouns. They will drag down your prose and puzzle your reader. Sentences containing nominalizations may be grammatically and factually correct, but they will almost certainly be vague and boring. Your reader will embrace your message more readily when it is built with verbs that animate your writing. Action verbs give life and energy to your prose. *Always*, when constructing a sentence and given the choice between a verb and a noun to help express your thoughts, choose the verb.

2.4 Footnotes

Samuel Johnson, generally referred to as "Dr. Johnson," was an 18th Century British author who contributed significantly to English literature as an essayist, playwright, poet, editor, literary critic, biographer and lexicographer. One of his noteworthy accomplishments was assembling a complete and accurate collection—a folio—of William Shakespeare's timeless plays, published in 1765. In the preface to his folio, Dr. Johnson condemned the use of footnotes in earlier collections of The Bard's works.

> Particular passages are cleared by notes, but the general effect of the work is weakened. *The mind is refrigerated by interruption*; the thoughts are diverted from the principal subject; the reader is weary, he suspects not why; and at last, throws away the book, which he has too diligently studied. (emphasis added)

Diverting the reader's eye from your primary message to a footnote, citing a judicial decision or learned treatise and providing a blurb explaining the need for the footnote is inexcusable. It does indeed *refrigerate* the reader's mind. Footnotes are like kicking sand in the reader's eye. Yet far too many judges and lawyers are afflicted with the urge to demonstrate their wisdom through the use of footnotes.

With judges leading the way, the past 40 years have witnessed an eruption in the use of footnotes, a stream of sludge contaminating cogent discourse. Below is an all-too-common example. An otherwise capable judge felt compelled to write two footnotes totaling 22 sentences, amplifying his thoughts in two sentences, as follows.

For this reason, this "half-life" formula—when it is used—is only appropriate for patients who took large amounts of a single dose (i.e., suicide attempts).[60] The literature applying "half-life" to determine dosage clearly states that this formula is only reliable for single ingestions. [61]

[60] This methodology was based on something called the Rumack-Matthews nonogram. See S. Flamm Dep., May 5, 2015 at 265 (Pl. Motion to Strike, Ex. 1). The nomogram, however, was not intended to be used for multiple or chronic dosing. See S. Flamm Dep., Apr. 8, 2016 at 261 (Doc. No. 206, Ex. E)("Q. Who is Dr. Rumack, to your knowledge? A. Dr. Rumack is a widely-known toxicologist who has published numerous articles in acetaminophen toxicity and liver failure and in fact is the author of the Rumack nomogram, which is used for body burden analysis and when to use N-acetylcysteine in patients with acetaminophen-related hepatotoxicity after a *single-point* ingestion. Very well-known

man in the field." (emphasis added)); J. Brent Dep., Mar. 30, 2016 at 57 (Doc. No. 206, Ex. D)("Q....You would agree with that, that the Rumack nomogram cannot be used for patients taking multiple doses of acetaminophen over multiple days, correct? A. That's correct, unless—unless the level is—with the one exception, with the level being high based on the time since the last dose, but that's not what it's designed to do, and that's not the way we generally use it. Q. Okay. So let me try that again. You would agree that the Rumack nomogram is to be used only in patients who have taken a single-point ingestion of acetaminophen at a known time, true? A. Based on—with the addition of that qualifier that I just gave, yes, that's true."). See also W. Lee Dep., Apr. 14, 2016 at 210–12 (Doc. No. 216, Ex. 3)("Q. Now, who is Barry Rumack? Let's go back 7 to that Exhibit 6. A. He—I think he started out life as a pediatrician, but he spent some time in the UK and the United—so did I. And in the UK in those early days—and he's—he's an older guy, as I am—that was where more paracetamol cases were found—that's acetaminophen, of course. And so he studied it a bit over there, and he came up with the so-called 'Rumack nomogram.'... He published the nomogram based upon scientific data that he holds—A. Yes. Yes. What year was that that he published the nomogram. Q. Probably in the '70s, correct? A. Yes. Q. And that nomogram that you referenced is used—was used at UTSMC, correct? A. Not very often. Q. No? Not in the emergency room? A. That—I don't know. I'm not an emergency room doctor. They—they may use it more than—more than I think. But it's not valuable very often. Q. The—the nomogram is used when the patient's brought in—first brought into the hospital in—in a potential single overdose case, correct? A. Yes. And they have to be a single overdose....They have to be a single overdose and the time of ingestion has to be known. Q.

And—A. Most cases that we see do not have either the exact time of ingestion. So it—it—or—or what—and as—as we've talked about with the unintentional cases, there's a lot of cases that are not a single time point. At least 50 percent are not a single time point. So—so the average hepatologist doesn't have much use for the Rumack nomogram, but I'm not—I'm not an ED doctor. I—it may be more commonly used there. Q. In other words, there may be clinicians of other stripes who use the nomogram more than a hepatologist. Fair? A. That's correct.") and at 368–69 (discussing same).

[61] See James, et al., "Pharmacokinetics of Acetaminophen-Protein Adducts in Adults with Acetaminophen Overdose and Acute Liver Failure," Drug Metabolism and Disposition, Vol. 37, No. 8, 1779–1784, 1782 (2009) (Doc. No. 206, Ex. S)("The Rumack nomogram, based on the measurement of APAP concentrations in peripheral blood relative to the reported time of overdose, is used in the clinical setting (e.g., emergency departments) to assess the risk of developing toxicity following acute APAP overdose. It is the cornerstone of evaluation and management for patients with *single, time-point ingestions who present within 24 h of APAP overdose* (Rumack et al., 1981; Rumack, 2002). However, beyond the acute stages of APAP toxicity, or in patients with unclear histories regarding the time of the overdose or ingestions at multiple time points, the utility of the Rumack nomogram is limited." (Emphasis added)).

Try wrapping your brain around that: Two footnotes totaling 752 words are supposedly necessary to explain two sentences totaling 43 words.

One highly regarded wordsmith was the late Robert Clifford, a New Jersey Supreme Court Justice. He, too, was baffled by the use of footnotes. In 1993, in a concurring opinion involving an attorney ethics matter, Justice Clifford lamented the use of footnotes:

> The Court's otherwise-impeccable opinion relegates to footnote status an important observation [the discussion of a recommendation of the Advisory Committee on Professional Ethics] ... And so, the footnote in the Court's opinion represents yet another setback in my woefully-ineffectual campaign to abolish footnotes from our opinions.... I deplore resort to footnotes not only in this case in particular but in judicial opinions generally. They distract. They cause the reader to drop the eyes; to absorb what is usually a monumental piece of irrelevancy or pseudo-scholarship but is sometimes—as here—a significant pronouncement that rightly belongs in the text; and then to return, without skipping a beat, to the point of departure on the upper part of the page. The whole irritating process points up the soundness of John Barrymore's observation that "[reading footnotes is] like having to run downstairs to answer the doorbell during the first night of the honeymoon," *quoted in* Norrie Epstein, *The Friendly Shakespeare* 75 (1992). *In re Opinion 662 Ethics Advisory* 133 N.J. 22 (1993)

Another judge sharing Justice Clifford's concern is Judge Beth Labson Freeman (U.S. District Court, California) who ordered a law firm to file a revised brief of no more than 25 pages without a single footnote. The judge's standing order provided that footnotes "are to be used sparingly and citations to textual matter shall not be used in footnotes." Yet every page of the plaintiffs' offending brief "contains at least two—and, on one page, eight—footnotes. The lines consumed by single-spaced footnotes outnumber the lines of double-spaced text on nearly half of the brief's pages."[11] Judge Labson Freeman was having none of it. She chastised the tone-deaf lawyer and required him to submit a new brief. Unfortunately, in recent years the plethora of footnotes in judicial opinions has granted lawyers license to do the same.

If a law review article, scientific treatise, or court's decision is so important that it warrants discussion in your brief, why can't it be included in the body of the brief? I see nothing that needs saying in a footnote that cannot be incorporated into the primary text. A small investment in time will keep the reader's eye gliding from one thought to the next. The more effort invested in your writing, the less effort required of your reader.

Finally, as to "source notes" versus footnotes: As you will notice, source notes appear in this text. Source notes are a far cry from footnotes. Source notes are there for the benefit of the curious reader interested in the "who and/or what" the author has relied upon as sources for quotes, opinions or authority. A source note does not command the reader's eye to go to the bottom of the page to read everything from a sentence to several paragraphs. Source notes are compiled at the rear of this handbook and merely reveal to studious/inquisitive readers where the author found the information mentioned in the text.

Part Two

STYLE & FUNDAMENTALS OF EFFECTIVE WRITING

*Atticus told me to delete the adjectives
and I'd have the facts.*

—Harper Lee

Chapter Three

STYLE & ORGANIZING YOUR THOUGHTS

Contents

3.1 Why is Style Important?

Why is style important? In the law, as in life, you only get one chance to make a first impression. People you may never meet—judges, lawyers and litigants—can form an opinion of you based upon a single document you have prepared. You need that opinion to be favorable. Lawyers build their reputations one interaction at a time. Every time you send out a written communication, you want the recipient to respect what you have to say. Yet to develop an effective style, you must apply yourself diligently. "The art of being brief; of touching heavy subjects with a light hand; and of sparing all superfluous detail does not come by nature to all those who have something which is well worth writing."[1]You believe your writing is important or you wouldn't be reading this book. Persist, and you will develop an effective writing style.

What is style? Style is the skillful use of words to engage the mind of the reader. You have broad freedom in stating your propositions. What delivers your message most powerfully is what matters. "Proper words in proper places make the true definition of style."[2] The choices you make, the words you select, and the construction of your sentences and paragraphs, all contribute to style. Skillful writers know that language must be bent to the needs of the audience and the age in which we live. No one style is correct or superior because effective use of language by attorneys is not subject to standards from on high. "Every style is good save that which bores."[3]

What defines effective style? Three traits: **(1)** the ability to distinguish between the words and structure that enhance your message versus those that may impede its delivery; **(2)** the ability to deploy syntax, diction and rhythm to ensure your message flows, is understood and is memorable and **(3)** the ability to craft sentences and paragraphs that engage your readers and prompt them to ponder your message. Finally, it's all about expressing your thoughts in a manner that permits them to be understood effortlessly by your reader. "The greatest merit of style is, of course, to make the words absolutely disappear into the thought."[4]

Lawyers play multiple roles as they make themselves understood on behalf of their clients, frequently serving as storytellers, teachers and advocates. As professional writers, we often play these three roles alternately and in unison. A lawyer's style is a key component of his ability to persuade others to embrace their client's position. Effective writing style improves a lawyer's ability to persuade in three ways: *first,* effective style guarantees that you will get your point across to your readers and that they won't waste time trying to figure out what it is you have to say; *second,* style brings a sense of dignity to the issues at hand and elevates the discussion; and *third,* style ingratiates you with the reader. When your readers see that your prose follows the rules of the English language, is accurate, consistent, and free of punctuation and spelling errors, you earn their trust. Instinctively, they know you are unlikely to mislead them on the facts or misstate the law. Admittedly, not every legal issue you address is profound, but that doesn't alter the fact that the issues involved are important to your client.

Despite my tenet that "less is more," that's not true on every occasion. It should always be your goal to "[e]xpress yourself clearly in plain, simple English using as few words as possible. [yet] To write for mere utility is as foolish as to dress for mere utility."[5] Sometimes more words are needed to embellish the facts in a dramatic, humorous or thought-provoking fashion. Other times, fewer but just the right words will hit the bullseye. Injecting a bit of self-denigrating or respectful humor, providing details highlighting conduct, or creating a touch of drama are all ways of setting your writing apart. During my years in private practice, I once filed a brief in support of sanctions, where I recounted the repeated, flagrant perjury of a witness at a deposition. Early in my pleadings, I quoted *Big Daddy,* the patriarch in Tennessee Williams' play, "Cat on a Hot Tin Roof." When confronted with a series of lies by family members, Big Daddy bellowed, *"There ain't nothin' more powerful than the odor of mendacity!"* [6]

In developing an effective writing style, you want your writing to "sound" like you, as if you were speaking at an oral argument or making a presentation to a client. Whatever approach works best for you and delivers the message most powerfully is what counts. "There is no style store; style is organic to the person doing the writing..."[7] Professional communicators understand that their language must not only be appropriate for the occasion but must be geared to the particular needs of the audience. Thus, each message matters, and when you write, you must always be mindful of *who* you are writing to, *why* and *what* you hope to achieve. An additional consideration is tone.

As discussed in Chapter Four, *tone* is an important ingredient often overlooked when discussing style. Your tone is the attitude or atmosphere your words convey, particularly when speaking. Tone can play a critical role in how your reader receives your message. Tone in writing cannot be as effortlessly achieved as tone in speech. "A writer cannot 'drip sarcasm' by anything as simple as modulating the voice. In writing, you have to change what you say. Choice of words, length of sentence, rhythm, and punctuation all contribute to the atmosphere in which ideas exist. They express an attitude toward the subject."[8] Effective communication requires you to find your own voice and then refine it until, subject to editing and revisions, all your writings sound like you when spoken aloud. Yet, "[s]peaking and writing involve very different kinds of human relationship, and only the one associated with speech comes naturally to us."[9] Because of how our brains are hardwired, you must recognize that attaining harmony between your spoken and written voice may require a concerted effort. Persist, and when you will get there, both your voices will be enhanced.

What makes a style interesting? Stated simply: economy of language, the variety of your diction and the vigor of your prose. Moreover, style becomes especially interesting when what you have to say is presented in a compelling, engaging and pithy manner. As Ernest Hemingway once said, "Any story is a great story if it is told well." As exemplified by Hemingway, if you want your words to matter, the fewer you use, the better. It's been my experience that the right words impact the force of your message in inverse relationship to their number.

Wise writers seeking to increase the power of their message occasionally make use of important literary works and quotes by historic figures. Noted trial lawyer Gerry Spence once said that "the quotes and quips of others provide raisins for our oatmeal."[10] As an attorney, your approach toward your writing style must be like the chef working in a restaurant in which the owner stocks the pantry based upon a budget, without consulting with his chef. You take the ingredients, assemble them on your kitchen table, and what's there is what you work with, aided by your creative instincts. Style is indeed very personal, but as a well-educated critical thinker, you will develop a writing style that sounds like your manner of speech.

Finally, with regard to style and everything you write, you must ask this question: "...[D]o these words, does this paragraph, does this entire piece, suit my present purpose? The purpose at large is always the same; it is to be understood aright. Reader and writer have both wasted their time if mental darkness is the only result of their separate efforts."[11] This is the standard for all your writing; "the reader's part of the effort must never become a strain."[12]

3.2 Creating a "Lead" (a/k/a Preliminary Statement)

This is the challenging part, where you begin to shape your message. At the outset, when advocating a client's position, you must tell your readers (or listeners) the *what* and the *how* of their situation and *where* you plan to take them. Whether writing an opinion letter to your client, an important memo to a colleague outlining your position, or a brief filed with the court in connection with a motion for summary judgment, you must lead with your position distilled to its essence. As stated by New Jersey's own, Albert Einstein, "If you can't explain it simply, you don't understand it well enough."

You can select the metaphor: a mug in which to pour your favorite craft beer, a landscaping plan to showcase a new home or the chassis for a restored antique automobile. Your goal is to concisely establish the framework for all that follows, and why your thoughts on the circumstances at hand are correct. To do that, you need to start with the optimal number of short, simple declaratory sentences that will: **(1)** logically support your overall message, **(2)** inform your audience of the appropriate end result, and **(3)** begin to persuade them on the issues that matter most. The more matter-of-factly you can do this—free of name-calling, hyperbole or lecturing on the law—the better. At this stage, the law is secondary. You are seeking to woo your readers with the facts, not alienate them by arguing. Acclaimed author and writing professor John McPhee uses the term "lead" (some writers use the term "lede") and refers to it as "the hardest part of a story to write." As expressed by McPhee, "All leads — of every variety—should be sound. They should never promise what does not follow. The lead should be a flashlight that shines down into the story. A lead is a promise."[13] The pledge you are making to your reader is "...that the piece of writing is going to be like this...[a]n integral beginning that sets a scene and implies the dimension of the story."[14]

Beginning any story, message or argument can be challenging. Your lead or preliminary statement—regardless of the label, if any—is where you lay the groundwork for convincing your reader that your position is faithful to the relevant facts.

There is no substitute for mastering the facts. The essential facts, boiled down to a sober, no-nonsense remnant that proclaims your position in terms that cannot be misconstrued, is where you must start. Though your client may not have been dealt a great hand on the crucial facts, that doesn't prevent you from presenting those facts in the best light possible. Even when the facts are lousy, and you may indeed have a losing position, your adversary will respect your efforts. She may be inclined to take you more seriously (or possibly be concerned by the points you have raised), enhancing your client's position to resolve things more favorably. Strong leads matter.

As you begin your analysis towards the preparation of your lead, take aim at the keywords, those terms essential to the correct telling of your story. It can be anything from a contract dispute or slip-and-fall personal injury claim, to a complex products liability mass tort involving pharmaceuticals. Upon concluding a careful analysis of your facts, you must then isolate the 5-7-10 terms that neither side can dispute are relevant to the matter at hand. If you have gathered all the essential facts, it's likely that you will have a greater number of terms than needed. Then ask yourself: **(1)** What is this matter all about? **(2)** What terms or phrases best describe the terrain everyone is on together? and **(3)** What are the concerns or issues everyone agrees are vitally important, regardless of their perspective on the needed outcome? Then use those terms like posts and planks of wood in a fence you are erecting, a fence everyone agrees contains all the needed materials and creates a cogent narrative that stands upon and neatly encircles the relevant facts. That's your goal. Although the readers of your lead may disagree with *where* you plan to take them, you must state the *what* and *how* of the events in question in a manner that leaves little room for dispute.

You may be writing the first paragraph of a memo to a new client confirming your understanding of the problem, a letter to your adversary informing her of the conditions necessary to resolve a dispute or a pre-trial brief with the judge presiding in your case. You should always strive to communicate your thoughts—in written form—in the same way you would hope to speak were your audience seated across the table from you. However, in this instance, you can edit your words. Your objective must always be to express your client's position as simply as possible. Yet, you also need to inject a degree of urgency, intensity and purposefulness, the same as if you were speaking one-to-one. It's advocacy, but subtle, restrained and thoughtful. The thought process for constructing your message is multi-faceted. You must not only think about the key terms chosen and how they are arranged, but also the maximum number of words you need to deliver your message. Lack of a coherent and concise format will sap your position of its vitality.

Syntax plays a large role in coherence and crafting a cogent statement. Strunk and White tell us that, "Confusion and ambiguity result when words are badly placed."[15] Examples of confusing/ambiguous writing versus cogent prose are provided below.

- Expecting a witness, the lawyer noticed a large man as he entered the courtroom and took his seat in the first row, hoping this was the person. (confusing)

versus

As the lawyer entered the courtroom, he noticed a large man seated in the first row and hoped this was the witness he was expecting. (cogent)

• Judge Smith, in his opinion, wrote about the consequences of the long history of discrimination and the impact of white males feeling entitled to positions of authority. (confusing)

versus

In his opinion, Judge Smith wrote about white males feeling entitled and the consequences of a long history of discrimination limiting who could gain positions of authority. (cogent)

In pursuit of coherence and cogency, you want the first and final sentence of each paragraph to include a strong word or phrase that emphasizes a point you need to make in building your argument. As illustrated by the two paragraphs below, the placement of emphatic words can make all the difference in the flow of your writing and its impact on the reader's eye. Note the difference between the two approaches to presenting the same essential facts on behalf of plaintiffs in a workplace gender discrimination claim. The statements utilize the same six terms: Borgata Babes, personal appearance, violation, sexual stereotyping, sex object and physically fit.

• The personal appearance standards required by defendant of plaintiffs, as Borgata Babes result in sexual stereotyping in violation of the law. It is one thing to be required to be physically fit, and quite another to be a sex object forced to work in a hostile work environment. (weak)

versus

"Borgata Babes" was the moniker foisted upon plaintiffs when told to remain physically fit. As enforced by defendant, the personal appearance standards are unlawful sexual stereotyping, rendering female workers sex objects, and creating a work environment that is hostile. (strong)

When you begin the first sentence of each paragraph with a strong word, you create energy in your prose. If you hope to capture your reader's eye you must begin with a noun, verb or adjective. It might be the name of a pivotal witness, a term integral to the storyline, or a glaring problem in need of explanation or ripe for exploitation. As you write, think of the period at the end of each sentence as a stop sign. "That slight pause in reading magnifies the final word, an effect intensified at the end of the paragraph where final words often adjoin white space. In a column of type, a reader's eyes are likewise drawn to the words next to the white space. Those words shout, "'Look at me!'"[16] That's why you must try to begin and end each sentence of your preliminary statement with a strong word that asserts some degree of emphasis. Depending upon the situation, the length of your lead may be as short as 30–40 words or as long as 150–300 words. As you rewrite and finalize your statement, omit needless words. Settling upon a word budget in advance will make your task easier by providing limits. Initially, you may find writing with a word budget to be constraining, but over time you will find it liberating.

Below are three sets of key terms and openers (leads) incorporating those terms. Each opposing statement is less than 40 words.

Contract Dispute—Key terms: performance, provided, breach, entitled, penalty, manager, consideration, understanding.

Buyer provided valuable <u>consideration</u> and is <u>entitled</u> to full <u>performance</u>. When under oath, seller's <u>manager</u> will not dispute our position. Seller's <u>breach</u> of the parties' <u>understanding</u> requires payment of the prescribed <u>penalty</u>.

Seller provided substantial <u>performance</u> in <u>compliance</u> with the parties' <u>understanding</u>. Seller's <u>manager</u> has opined that the <u>consideration</u> tendered was sub-par. The <u>breach</u> is minor and buyer is not entitled to payment of a <u>penalty</u>.

Slip and fall—Key terms: wet, unlit, stairway, handrail, exterior, fall and guest.

<u>Unlit</u> <u>exterior</u> <u>stairways</u> are dangerous. My client was a <u>guest</u> of your tenant and was trying to reach the apartment when she slipped on <u>wet</u> steps. The <u>handrail</u> was missing several screws and broke loose causing her to <u>fall</u>.

<u>Exterior</u> <u>stairways</u> and <u>handrails</u> are subject to the weather and can become <u>wet</u>. Your client was not a lawful <u>guest</u> at the property, nor was it <u>unlit</u>. Had your client exercised reasonable care she would not have <u>fallen</u>.

Products liability/pharmaceutical claim—Key terms: FDA, label, consumer, "America's Number One Pain Reliever," warning, illness, and side-effects.

Despite <u>FDA</u> approval many years ago, the manufacturer's <u>label</u> wasn't amended to provide a <u>warning</u> that the <u>illness</u> experienced by plaintiff, the <u>consumer</u>, was one of the potential <u>side-effects</u> of what is sold as "<u>America's</u> <u>Number One Pain Reliever</u>."

> FDA's <u>label</u> approval for "<u>America's Number One Pain Reliever</u>" was granted 50 years ago. The <u>illness</u> purportedly experienced by your client was one of the potential <u>side-effects</u> covered by a common sense reading of the approved <u>consumer warning</u>.

Depending upon the nature of the situation, the complexity of the issues and how well you know the facts—or don't—crafting an effective preliminary statement may take a few minutes, or several hours of writing, editing and rewriting. Rewriting is always time well spent. Crafting a sound, potent and eye-catching lead is an investment capable of paying dividends far into the future. A month, a year, a decade later, all you will need do is re-read your preliminary statement and you will recall nearly everything that you thought you had forgotten about the matter. No matter the occasion, writing a powerful lead is an investment in time you will never regret.

3.3 Word Budgets

Word budgets are essential for everything you write. You need to make it part of your routine to create a budget for the number of words needed to express your thoughts on a given situation. As discussed at the outset, lawyers' communications are part of the "attention economy," and your message must be tailored to float to the surface among a torrent of random information, sales pitches and rubbish. If you fail to craft a tight message, you risk the reader concluding that what you've written is too long, and unworthy of the required investment in time. All your efforts in crafting your message may be ignored simply because of its length.

After you've gathered the relevant facts, and have a firm grasp of the issues, as well as your audience, decide on the minimum number of words required to express your thoughts on the issues at hand? What follows are proposed guidelines for the creation of word budgets:

1. **Emails**: 200–250 words. For many lawyers, emails are the principal means of communicating with colleagues, clients and, often, government officials. *First*, never send an email without proofreading it. *Second*, if you need more than 250 words to express yourself in an email, and don't want to write a formal letter, then prepare a memo and send it as an attachment with a brief explanation of what the attachment contains. *Third*, remember the forward button. A hasty email sent without giving it adequate thought can come back to haunt you.

2. **Routine Letters**: 300–500 words. Whether to a client, colleague or the court, letters of more than two pages are unwelcome by most recipients. To a large extent—for the better—emails have replaced lawyers' routine letters. Thus, when you decide to prepare a letter on law firm stationery, you should have something important to say. If you want your letter to be read, choose your words carefully and boil down your message to its basics. When you send a letter via email, always do so as an attachment, with a short, explanatory statement.

3. **Opinion Letters**: 3,000 words. Lawyers are often called upon to express formal opinions on diverse issues. Frequently, lawyers err on the side of trying to address every contingency. *Don't!* Focus on the issues essential to ar-

riving at a conclusion that addresses the client's concerns. A word budget of 3,000 (seven to nine double-spaced pages) is ample to express an opinion. If you are concerned about leaving out something critical, consider attaching exhibits amplifying your opinion, or listing unanswered questions.

4. **Routine Memos**: 1,500–2,500 words. Associates write memos for partners and partners use them to make decisions in advising clients. A word budget of 1,500-2,500 (six to eight double-spaced pages) provides interested readers sufficient information to make preliminary decisions. If more research is required, the memo can be expanded; let your reader know that.

5. **Preamble to a Contract**: 250–500 words. As discussed in Chapter Six, Rule #1 for every lawyer responsible for preparing an agreement is to *know your deal*. If you have a full understanding of the transaction, 500 words is ample.

6. **Routine Legal Brief**: 4,000 words. Whether a motion involving unanswered discovery, a petition to compel a deposition or a request for a date certain for a trial, a word budget of 4,000 words (10–11 double-spaced pages) will usually suffice.

7. **Legal Brief on Summary Judgment**: 7,500 or less words. This is my favorite. During my time on the bench, I frequently saw briefs in connection with motions for summary judgment that, *sans* exhibits, exceeded 40 pages, more than 13,000 words. Most of those briefs were hundreds of sentences too few, and thousands of words too many. A long chapter in a serious work of history

contains 7,500 words. No matter how complex, learn to distill your argument to the finer points.

These guidelines for word budgets are only suggestions. That said, seasoned attorneys who respect their audience likely adhere to similar word budgets. If you wish to avoid losing your reader because what you've written is too long, you will do your best to adhere to these suggested word budgets.

Chapter Four

DEVELOPING YOUR WRITING STYLE: BLOCK I

Contents

Introduction

A writer must touch many bases in order to develop an effective writing style. Issues such as syntax, diction, rhythm and linking shouldn't be sprinkled throughout this handbook. So here, and in Chapter Five, are suggestions for developing your own writing style. My goal for you is writing that is lean, strong and free of embellishment. What is an apt metaphor for simple unadorned prose? Black and white movies. Think of *To Kill a Mockingbird*, *Casablanca* or *Schindler's List*. Think of how powerful those movies are. Many popular songs also provide examples of lyrics that are lean, strong and free of embellishment.

Think of Carole King and *You've Got a Friend*, Bill Withers and *Lean on Me* and, finally, The Beatles' *Let it Be*. More than 75 percent of the words in each song are one syllable.

4.1 Syntax

What is *syntax*? As defined by the Oxford English Dictionary, syntax is "The arrangement of words and phrases to create well-formed sentences in a language." The word "syntax" comes from the Ancient Greek word "syntaxis," meaning "coordination" or "ordering together." Indeed, the ordering of your words in a pleasing manner, ensuring clarity, is what this handbook is all about. Fundamentally, syntax is about structure. The rules of syntax exist to make sentences clear, consistent and easily understood, as noted by Strunk & White:

> The position of the words in a sentence is the principal means of showing their relationship. Confusion and ambiguity result when words are badly placed. The writer must, therefore, bring together the words and group of words that are related in thought and keep apart those that are not...The subject of a sentence and the principal verb should not as a rule, be separated by a phrase or clause that can be transferred to the beginning.[1]

Because nearly all the rules for writing in the English language can be broken, and still yield writing with a pleasing style, what follows are four standards grammarians generally agree upon with regard to the construction of sentences and syntax.

1. <u>Subject-Verb-Object</u> ("SVO") Pattern: This is the most fundamental syntactic structure. In addition to a subject ("S") and verb ("V") the other potential elements include the direct object ("O"), indirect object ("IO"), complement ("C") and adverb ("A"). There are seven patterns for the SVO structure. At a minimum, they must include a subject and verb. (i) S + V: *The witness cried.* (ii) S + V + O: *The witness described the exhibit.* (iii) S + V + IO + O: *The witness handed the lawyer the exhibit.* (iv) S + V + C: *The witness oozed confidence.* (v) S + V + C: *The witness spoke well.* (vi) S + V + O + C: *The witness returned the exhibit wrinkled.* (vii) S + V + O + A: *The witness carefully wrote her initials on the exhibit.*

2. <u>Simple Declaratory Statement</u>: This structure generally dominates effective writing style. In nearly all these sentences, your clause contains a subject and the subject precedes a verb, and there is often an object. (E.g., The witness described the exhibit.)

3. <u>Questions</u>: There are three principal types of questions: (i) yes or no questions; (ii) who/what/where/when/how questions and (iii) alternative questions, providing options. Additionally, there are questions pertaining to: (a) having the structure of a declaratory statement (e.g., *You're starting your trial on Monday?),* (b) tag questions (e.g., *You've prepared for tomorrow's deposition, didn't you?)* and (c) exclamatory questions (e.g), *Just how wonderful was the jury's verdict?).*

4. <u>Parallel Structure</u>: Parallelism is the repetition of the same grammatical form in two or more parts of a sen-

tence. Maintaining parallel structure improves your writing style and helps you avoid grammatically incorrect sentences. Sentences with parallel structure are easier to read and add a sense of balance to your writing. Where this generally comes into play is in addressing thoughts with a series of items or verbs. (E.g., (a) *The law firm wants to hire someone who is personable, intelligent, organized and punctual.* **versus** ... *is personable, intelligent, organized and arrives to work on time.* [not parallel] (b) *The witness was emphasizing nonsense, exaggerating and lying.* **versus** ... *emphasizing nonsense, exaggerating and told lies* [not parallel] (c) *The lawyer quoted from a statute, cited the rule book and opined on the case law.* **versus** ... *quoted from a statute, cited to the rule book and put forth his thoughts on the case law.* [not parallel].)

What follows are three simple rules that will help you with syntax. *First,* strive to consistently use the active voice. In English, a strong, active voice sentence will ordinarily have the subject doing the action of the sentence. Avoid the passive voice unless it is absolutely necessary. The active voice keeps the flow of your thoughts moving forward; the passive voice usually results in a digression that often can confuse your reader. *Second,* it's all about the sentences you write. Never lose sight of the fact that, "Sentences should be built like good fences, every word solidly in place, and each giving strength to all the others."[2] You build your message one sentence at a time. *Third,* as discussed in Chapter Seven, any serious piece of writing is best edited "cold." Edit your writing by reading it aloud. Whether you mumble quietly or read your writing aloud to yourself, your ear can identify syntactical problems in your sentences your eye will miss.

Before moving on, it's helpful to illustrate the problem posed by the passive voice and the need for the active voice.

Passive: The order was issued by Justice Roberts.

Active: Justice Roberts issued the order.

Passive: The bill was not acted upon because of Congress's refusal to act.

Active: Congress refused to act on the bill.

Passive: The verdict was delivered by the jury foreman's answers to the judge's questions.

Active: The jury foreman delivered the verdict by answering the judge's questions.

In each instance, the active voice aids the reader not only by creating movement but also by creating an image, helping the reader to visualize what occurred.

4.2 Diction

Diction is the choice and use of words and phrases in speech or writing. Diction and syntax focus on related concerns. Syntax focuses on the order and structure of words, while diction focuses on word choice. Why is diction important? Mark Twain said it best: "The difference between the almost right word and the right word is really a large matter. 'Tis the difference between the lightning bug and the lightning." Always be attentive to the vocabulary that courses through your writing, and in all the things you read. "[I]t is not enough to pay attention to words only when you face the task of writing—that is like playing the violin only on the night of the concert. You must attend to words when you read, when you speak, when others speak."[3]

Diction depends on **subject, purpose and audience**. Your subject generally drives the agenda regarding how sophisticated or focused your diction needs to be. For example, a legal brief on an indemnification claim against a guarantor arising out of faulty construction will need to address terms specific to the insurance and contracting business. Such topics often have special vocabularies. The same holds true for specialized matters such as those involving medical malpractice, product liability, intellectual property, etc. Each has its own jargon. Yet use no more than necessary to address the issues at hand.

Purpose also influences a lawyer's diction. Words chosen to convey a particular effect on the reader reflect the writer's purpose. If your purpose is to inform the reader, your diction should be straightforward, guided by the issues. On the other hand, if your purpose is to send a message that negotiations are at the end of the line, a lawyer may need to deploy words that are conclusory or confrontational.

Finally, the type of diction an attorney uses depends on her audience. Whether writing to the court, an adversary or lay people, an attorney must tailor his language accordingly. At the end of the day, be ever mindful that lawyers are judged by their words. A pint of well-chosen words is an anvil upon which to hammer home your argument; a gallon of the cleverest words can turn your argument into mush.

Let's address the choice of "just the right word." This problem is easier to resolve today than it was 30 years ago. If your computer doesn't provide convenient access to a dictionary and thesaurus, then make the necessary upgrades to ensure that it does. The online versions of the Oxford English Dictionary ("OED") and the Merriam Webster's Dictionary are excellent tools for professional writers. The ability to quickly nail down the meaning of a term, or find a replacement word where the repeated use of a word is growing weary to the "reader's eye," can markedly enhance the quality of your writing.

Diction becomes wearisome when lawyers fail to notice the frequency with which they use a term in a single document. In addition to regular use of a dictionary and thesaurus, utilize the "find" tool of your software to identify the number of times and locations particular words appear in your draft document. As part of your final review and editing, make it a habit to use the "find" tool for key words in your argument. If you see particular terms central to your message are used too frequently, use your thesaurus to find suitable replacement words to keep your audience from becoming bored. A lawyer who fails to make regular use of a dictionary, thesaurus, and the find tool is akin to a chef cooking without seasonings. To conclude on diction, find the "lightning" urged by Mark Twain, and never overuse a word or phrase.

4.3 Rhythm (or "Cadence")

What does rhythm mean in writing? Rhythm, or cadence, is the pattern of stresses within a line of prose; it is the flow of words within a literary work. The placement of words in relation to one another determines whether or not the rollout of your words is pleasing. This movement of language is primarily created through diction (i.e., your choice of words and syntax, and how you choose to arrange those words).

How does rhythm work? One way to define rhythm is "The measured flow of words and phrases in verse or prose as determined by the relation of long and short or stressed and unstressed syllables."[4] In writing, rhythm is defined by punctuation and the stress patterns of various words in a sentence, namely those words you wish to emphasize; long sentences may sound smoother and more elegant, while short sentences can make your content snappier. You must deploy both. When you permit each sentence, or paragraph, to follow the same structure and rhythm, your writing will quickly become boring. In short, you must mix things up to keep the reader's eye moving across the page. Avoid two long sentences or paragraphs followed by another. Never permit three in a row. What is a "long" sentence? In this paragraph, the third sentence deploys 41 words to define rhythm. Ordinarily, that's approaching the outer limits. What's a short sentence? The sentence that follows the longest sentence in this paragraph is five words.

Here are three suggestions for enhancing your rhythm. **(1) Alternate the length of your sentences.** Vary the word count for your sentences, sometimes by counting the number of words, but always naturally. On occasion, that may require adding words to the fragments of a long sentence that must be broken up. Don't be afraid to use a well-contrived run-on sentence, followed by an artful short sentence of fewer than 10 words, much like snapping your fingers. **(2)** Reposition words and phrases: "English is a flexible language. Exploit that fact. Though parts of speech have set interrelationships, the relative positions of words representing the categories are negotiable. Shift words and phrases around until the parts of a sentence seem to fall into their preordained places."[5] **(3)** Utilize sentence fragments. Concerns over incomplete sentences died a long time ago. Most people frequently speak in incomplete sentences and fragments.

You can too. Employed judiciously, sentence fragments can highlight issues and excite the rhythm of your writing.

Ditto, as to contractions. *Don't, doesn't, isn't, won't, can't*, etc. are all acceptable when used sparingly, and placed prudently. All that said, your writing must consistently convey carefully constructed thoughts.

4.4 Tone & Style

There is an important difference between simplicity and informality. Simplicity is your goal in every communication. Yet, it's the rare occasion that a lawyer communicates informally when writing to a client or colleague, and never to a judge. Informality has no place in communications in which you are writing or speaking as an attorney.

Clarity, lucidity and directness should be foremost in your mind as you begin preparing any business-related dispatch, and before those qualities comes candor. Whether or not you are involved in litigated matters. You are always an officer of the court, sworn to an oath that all your statements will be truthful. Casual, nonchalant or less than candid statements are unacceptable from a member of the bar. Truth must be ever-present in all you write and speak. Yet formal communications with your clients or colleagues cannot all have the same tone of formality. You need to select words that will unmistakably signal your intentions to your reader. Something I learned from my first mentor that applies to everything you write, especially letters and emails, is the need to set the tone from the first sentence. You need to tell your reader precisely and concisely where you are headed and why.

The 12 examples below illustrate recurring exchanges with colleagues for which the correct tone ought to be set in your very first sentence, *always* expressed in less than 15 words.

Acceptance: You will be pleased to learn that we accept your proposal of (_____date).

Rejection: Unfortunately, we are unable to accept your proposal of (_____date).

Urgency: It's important that you give this matter your prompt attention.

Opposition: We respect your position but will resist it with all our energy.

Ultimatum: The position outlined below is not negotiable.

Support: I wholeheartedly embrace your position.

Skepticism: Your position is not supported by the facts of this matter.

Willingness to negotiate: We remain hopeful that this matter can be amicably resolved.

Hostilities to come: Our negotiations have been exhausted; litigation is necessary.

Confidence in prevailing: There are no more cards to play; my client has the better hand.

Confidential: Absent my consent, nothing stated herein can be shared with anyone.

CYA a/k/a Cover Your Ass: I don't want to write this letter but events force me to do so.

The stronger your grasp of the facts and knowledge of the applicable law, the easier it is to begin your message with a forceful tone. One reason it is wise to set the tone from the very first sentence and send only short letters and emails is that too much information gives the person receiving it more to *mis*interpret. As discussed in Chapters Three and Seven, I recommend emails be limited to 200–250 words. If you have more to say, you should compose a formal letter or memorandum and attach it as a separate document. If your recipient hits the forward button, you want everyone who receives the submission to respect you.

4.5 Rule of Three & Tricolons

Omne trium perfectum is a Latin phrase meaning "Everything that comes in threes is perfect," or "every set of three is complete." This maxim of the Romans expresses the idea known as the "power of three" or the "rule of three." The rule of three is a principle of communicating that pre-dates the written word; it has existed as long as human society. Nearly every story is better told by using the rule of three. There are several reasons why the rule of three adds style to your message when organizing words to tell your story. Predictably, there are *three* rationales. *First*, rhythm—whether you term it tempo, pacing or cadence, rhythm is essential to engaging your reader. *Second*, every story or message of any importance needs a beginning, middle and end. Three feels solid and well-grounded to both our eyes and ears. *Third*, three is the smallest number from which a pattern can arise. Three common examples of patterns are: "Stop, Look and Listen." "*The Good, The Bad And The Ugly.*" And, finally, Julius Caesar's phrase, *Veni, Vidi, Vici* (I came, I saw, I conquered.)

In each instance, the sequence creates a reassuring and persuasive pattern.

Because reciting three terms, thoughts or phrases combines both brevity and rhythm with the least amount of information required to create a pattern, it makes your message simple and appealing. The rule of three makes your content more effective, satisfying and memorable. Three provides a sense of wholeness. Three is compelling. Generally, three nouns, adjectives or phrases linked together to explain something are more powerful than trying to reach the same understanding using four such terms. The fourth term gets in the way. It's a distraction that mutes your message. What's more, the rule of three can refer to anything from a collection of three words, phrases or sentences, to quotes, sections of statutes or names of acts of Congress. The three elements together are known as a *triad* and, also, a *tricolon*.

Tricolons are used effectively everywhere from prose, poetry and storytelling to films, photography and advertising. Many marketing campaigns use this technique to create a catchy, persuasive and indelible means of presenting information. It's no coincidence that some of the most enduring phrases in history are structured in three parts, *think*: faith, hope and charity; life, liberty and the pursuit of happiness; or Thomas Hobbes's view of man's life in the state of nature, "nasty, brutish and short." It all comes down to the way we humans process information. Humans have become proficient at pattern recognition by necessity, and three is the smallest number of elements required to create a pattern that implants itself in your audience's brain. If you want something to stay with your audience, put it in a sequence of three. To appreciate how common yet powerful tricolons are, consider the following examples.

1. Lincoln's speech at Gettysburg, which many historians view as a bridge between the Declaration of Independence and the U.S. Constitution, contains this tricolon: *"we cannot dedicate, we cannot consecrate, we cannot hallow this ground..."* He concludes with another memorable tricolon: *"Government of the People, by the People, for the People."*

2. President Dwight Eisenhower's speech, "Chance for Peace," makes excellent use of tricolons. *"Every gun that is made, every warship launched, every rocket fired* signifies, in the final sense, a theft from those who hunger and are not fed, those who are cold and are not clothed. The world in arms is not spending money alone. It is *spending the sweat of its laborers, the genius of its scientists, the hopes of its children."*

3. Martin Luther King Jr. also used the rule of three in many of his influential speeches. For example, the speech "Non-Violence and Racial Justice" contained a binary opposition made up of the rule of three: *"insult, injustice and exploitation,"* followed a few lines later by *"justice, good will and brotherhood."* Less gracefully (and unnecessarily confrontational), at the time of his inauguration, a contemporary of Dr. King, Alabama Governor George Wallace raged: *"segregation now, segregation tomorrow, segregation forever."*

Opportunities abound for the use of tricolons in your writing. Generally speaking, lawyers are educated in more than the law. Those seven years of schooling exposed you to a great deal of writing and endowed you with a rich vocabulary exceeding that of the average person. Make it your practice, as you analyze the issues you handle on a daily basis, to search for three logical components. When you have a thought you wish to convey, try visualizing a triangle, a three-legged stool, the face of a pyramid, etc. Then, work at breaking your thought into three of its principal *attributes, components* or *redeeming qualities* and use those terms to make your point more *cogently, forcefully* and *memorably* by stringing together words or phrases that add *meaning, texture* and *power.* (Note the trifecta of tricolons.)

Another aspect of rhythm that can add power is how you position multiple words and phrases used to explain an issue. Whether you deploy a tricolon or a string of words to modify or elaborate upon a concept, you need to be sensitive to the arrangement of those words. To make them pleasing to the reader, it's preferable that they *ascend,* where the length of words and phrases grow longer, or *descend,* where the length of words and phrases grow shorter as you expand upon your thought. Take note of their length and/or the number of syllables in those words. For example, look again at the quotes by Dr. King, which *ascend* as he proceeds: *insult, injustice and exploitation,* followed by *justice, goodwill and brotherhood.* Had he said, "insult, exploitation and injustice" and continued with "justice, brotherhood and goodwill," he would have impaired the rhythm and undermined his message. The same is true for President Eisenhower's speech in which his key phrases *descend* as he goes forward. Their styles are pleasing to both the eye and the ear. Also, when ranking the order of the phrases where some have the same number of words, count the number of syllables and/or the letters within the words and rank them accordingly, whether ascending (growing longer) or descending (grower shorter).

Consider the following examples of tricolons and their arrangement. As you do, scrutinize the placement of the individual phrases, taking note of the number of words (sometimes total syllables and/or letters) within those phrases. To attain cogency with style, those phrases must either *ascend*, that is, get larger/longer, or *descend*, that is get smaller/shorter. When you assemble the phrases without regard to the length of the individual phrases of your tricolon, you run the risk of being inharmonious to both the eye and ear.

Here are some examples:

- <u>Filing of a lawsuit</u>: Plaintiff's lawsuit not only attacks my client, it challenges our right to do business, and if successful will disrupt the status quo of an entire industry. (ascending)

- <u>Court order</u>: This court order incorporates the judge's ruling, issues a stern edict and mandates compliance. (descending)

- <u>Breach of contract</u>: By abandoning this contract, the seller shirked an obligation, violated a covenant and breached a solemn duty. (ascending)

- <u>Opinion letter</u>: This transaction poses multiple challenges to be recited in a future memo, creates an abundance of profit opportunities and will require significant financing. (descending)

4.6 Linking

Whether writing a settlement proposal to your adversary, a formal opinion letter to a worried client, or a detailed analysis of the deposition of your opponent's chief expert witness, the role of an attorney is comparable to that of a nonfiction essay writer.

The same is true when writing a brief. Much like an essayist, the lawyer must master the facts, focus upon the pivotal issues and identify the key terms necessary for an understanding of the issues at hand. It's vital for a lawyer's writing to always give the reader the feeling of moving forward. As shown in the passive voice versus active voice, movement helps your reader visualize your thoughts.

Movement is what distinguishes prose that is a pleasure to read from that which is boring. Movement is achieved by *linking*. In writing, linking is "a principle of construction... [I]t is an operation performed by words, phrases, and idioms, as well as by simple placing... [of words]."[6] *Linking* is taking syntax to the next level. Instead of sentences, we are addressing the structure of the entire document you are writing: sentence to sentence, paragraph to paragraph, page to page. Through proper linking, you will create a unified work that encourages the reader's eye to glide from one sentence to the next with little effort.

Lawyers, like nearly all of humanity, don't think in full sentences. Rather, we think in single words that correspond to half-formed ideas, "clusters of untrimmed ideas that must be taken apart and looked at to test their connections and to find the best order of setting them down."[7] The analogy of a sentence to a fence only takes us so far. With linking, we are creating a superstructure, akin to the framework of a building. Each post, beam and stud has a role to play in the message you are crafting. The connection between ideas in a sentence, paragraph or entire document generally depends upon the order in which they are arranged. Readers assume what they are reading at any given moment relates to what was read earlier. Forcing a reader to backtrack and reread a portion runs the risk of losing your reader. The flow of the facts you choose to highlight, and the arguments you present for consideration by your reader, must appear to progress seamlessly. Attention must be paid to how you move from one sentence to another and from the final sentence of a paragraph to the first sentence of the paragraph that follows. Try to include a strong, noticeable word in the last sentence of a paragraph that can be used in the first sentence of the following paragraph.

Each paragraph usually presents a new major point in support of the central thesis of your writing. "These points are not isolated ideas but rather aspects of the overall thought and should be connected."[8] I have read briefs that seem little more than a bunch of ideas splattered on the page, paragraphs raising different/unconnected issues one after another. "Well-constructed [briefs] read smoothly, continuously. Each paragraph is linked to the one before and the one after, like a series of connecting rods for transmitting power."[9] When your thoughts flow through your writing, gaining strength and momentum, the reader's eye will glide along.

Successful writers are critical thinkers and are sensitive to the momentum of their prose. Like an artist examining his colors and brush strokes, as you proceed with your writing take a step back to review your essay for its logical flow. With the essence of your message in mind, ask whether your paragraphs are truly consecutive. "When one paragraph makes a statement that will be developed in the next few paragraphs, check to be sure each one bears out the controlling statement. Look at the natural sections into which your essay falls—do they move consecutively, projecting from your thesis?"[10] Your final step is to see the essay as a cohesive whole. Is its flow unbroken? If not, remove the obstacles. Critical thinking focused on economy of language, word placement and diction can help you remove even the biggest obstacles. Consecutiveness (i.e., logical progression from one paragraph to the next), is essential to strong writing. Yet, just as there are ways to bind sentences from one paragraph to another, so there are ways to clarify and tighten the links between paragraphs on your march toward coherence.

4.7 Coherence

Coherent writing is your primary goal. Coherence, or clarity of expression, is created when correct vocabulary and grammar are used. Absent both coherence and cohesion, you run the risk of confusing your reader as a result of gaps in the thoughts presented. Writing that lacks coherence is difficult to read and understand. You defeat the entire purpose of your writing, which is to convey your thoughts in a clear and efficient style.

Coherence, and the reader's need for it, is what must drive the entire process of assembling words in delivering your message. Coherence begins with you and your reader being clear about the topic you wish to address. The reader must know the topic of your message, and it is "essential to let the reader in on the topic early."[11] As discussed in Chapter Three, your "lead" must let your reader know you are master of the facts and you are confident about where you are going and why. How you tie your ideas together is paramount. Strong sentences and paragraphs are critical. The words chosen to link your thoughts to each other make all the difference in being readily understood. A strong sentence hangs together solidly, as do your paragraphs, one to another. "One thought logically and naturally follows from the preceding thought and gives rise to the next. The sentences [and paragraphs] are locked to the other like the cars of a train."[12]

Coherence in writing is the logical linking of words, sentences and paragraphs through the use of connecting or transition words. Transition words are essential. They are integral to: **(1)** connecting ideas, **(2)** providing a contrast illuminating a thought and **(3)** introducing a needed shift in the direction of your prose. Transition words may also be used to: **(1)** display agreement, **(2)** emphasize a particular point or **(3)** highlight conclusions. Examples of transitional or connective words and phrases used to link ideas and thoughts are listed below. These words, separated into seven categories as to how they are generally deployed, are not exhaustive; you are only limited by your imagination.

1. Agreement, Similarity, Addition (indicate specific conditions or intentions): *furthermore, coupled with, similarly, yet, moreover, again, then, together with, not to mention, in the first place, also, first, second, third, comparatively, because of, due to, for the purpose of, so as to, in the hope that.*

2. Opposition, Limitation, Contradiction (indicate alternatives or information to the contrary): *but, yet, although, in contrast, then again, even though, besides, otherwise, on the contrary, albeit, regardless, despite, in spite of, conversely, above all, as much as, nevertheless, instead, at the same time.*

3. Condition, Cause, Purpose (indicate qualifying conditions or intentions): *unless, in the event that, when, given that, with this intention, so that, to the end that, because of, in as much as, since, in view of, while, due to, for fear that, whenever, so as to, so long as, even if, provided that, in case, in the hope that.*

4. Effect, Consequence, Result (indicate particular timing of an effect): *therefore, consequently, for, as a result, because*

the, in that case, then, forthwith, accordingly, under the circumstances, in effect, hence, thereupon, all the while, once again, for this reason, from that moment on, henceforth.

5. <u>Place, Location, Space</u> (indicate restrictions, limitations or qualification on space): *in the middle of, in front of, near, alongside of, below, beneath, in the center of, beyond, here and there, next to, adjacent to, nearby, above, besides, on this side, wherever, in the foreground, across.*

6. <u>Support, Examples, Emphasis</u> (indicate importance and/or illustrate related idea): *notably, in other words, like, namely, in particular, as an illustration, for this reason, chiefly, to demonstrate, with attention to, indeed, to reiterate, explicitly, by all means, first thing to remember, including, to enumerate, to be certain.*

7. <u>Conclusion, Summary, Restatement</u> (indicate that the matter is concluded and/or how): *after all, on balance, in a word, to summarize, ultimately, as can be seen, in brief, all in all, ordinarily, as shown above, in essence, by and large, in the final analysis, altogether, all things considered, in any event, to sum up.*

Thoughtful use of transition words will enable you to deliver your message free of: **(1)** confusing or misleading gaps in your prose, **(2)** embarrassing leaps in your argument and **(3)** major potholes in your writing. As you proceed in linking together your sentences and paragraphs, every thought supporting your argument must receive the appropriate emphasis. Each idea builds upon the one before it and gains power, one sentence, one paragraph and one page at a time, as you proceed to conclude your message. "When a paragraph is coherent, thoughts and ideas develop continuously, and the relationships are clear. The current of thought flows. There are no jerks, no backing, and filling, no long leaps from the period of one sentence to the capital letter of the next."[13] In short, no surprises. A coherent and cohesive text is one where the reader can effortlessly recognize the thematic consistency of your writing. Professional writers can never permit anything they write to be a source of confusion. Whether termed clearness, coherence or comprehensibility, a lawyer's words and their meaning must always be understood.

Chapter Five

DEVELOPING YOUR WRITING STYLE: BLOCK II

Contents

5.1 Seven Rules for Solid Composition

Discussed below are seven suggestions (a/k/a "rules") for improving your writing. They repeat some points made elsewhere but are bundled together here for those attorneys in search of the principal guideposts for improving their writing.

"Know where you are going" is always first. Never begin writing anything of substance without an outline. The 18 questions posed in Sections 5.1.1 and 5.1.2 are presented as guidance for every lawyer concerned about staying on a course consistent with their client's needs. The remaining five rules are essential to developing an effective writing style.

5.1.1 Know Where You are Going

You will write no better than you think. Lawyers with unclear thoughts are doomed to communicate unclearly. To be effective, your writing must reflect your thoughts, but not always in the order in which they initially occur to you. Before you begin to write, take time to think about the points you wish to make, the components comprising your message, and the priority of each element. If you begin with a fairly detailed outline, it is easier to understand the relevance of what you are writing in any given paragraph or section of your document. No matter how simple, effective writers begin with a roadmap, namely, an outline. Thus "...planning must be a deliberate prelude to writing. The first principle of composition is to foresee or determine the shape of what is to come and pursue that shape."[1] The more important the issue, complex the facts and intricate the legal standards, the more imagination, effort and time you must devote to devising a plan for your writing. Whether it be brief, letter or email, know with certainty what you want to say. Think it through. What's the content you hope to deliver?

As you develop your thoughts, ask yourself the following questions. **(1)** Why was I retained? **(2)** What are my client's chief concerns? **(3)** What are the principal issues that must be addressed? **(4)** What is an unacceptable result for my client? **(5)** Are there any controlling legal standards? **(6)** Are my client's goals "doable" under all the circumstances? Once you've answered these questions, along with the "who, what, when, where, why and how" of your circumstances, you are ready to write.

Refine your message to its core. Your first sentence (or two) should capture the essence of your message. Select simple words that fuse the fundamental aspects of what you are trying to communicate to the reader. Though writing is indeed all about sentences and ensuring each post and plank in your fences are faithful to your message, paragraphs are the building blocks of any substantial issue you wish to advance. Paragraphs are the essential units for conveying your thoughts. You must learn to link them to one another.

As advised by Strunk and White, "... begin each paragraph with a sentence that suggests the topic or with a sentence that helps the transition."[2] You should also work toward ending each paragraph with a sentence containing a strong word that reinforces the principal concern of that paragraph and leads the reader to the next element of your primary issue expressed in the following paragraph. Each of your paragraphs should present a new major point that supports your primary message. Yet, these new points are not isolated ideas; they are facets of your overall message, connected through the vitality of linking. It's critical that you sustain momentum. There must be a sense of movement and continuity. You create thematic coherence by continually refining, yet expanding your message, detailing new and vital aspects of your subject. Remove or transpose anything that interrupts the march of your thoughts. As you progress, regularly take a step back, with your thesis in mind, and ask yourself the following questions. **(1)** Is each paragraph bonded to the one before it? **(2)** Does the strength of my message gain momentum? **(3)** Have I said anything that can be misconstrued? **(4)** Have I omitted any key facts? **(5)** Do my thoughts flow smoothly and continuously?

When you are satisfied your text coherently addresses all the pertinent issues, you have a working draft document. Then you read and revise, and keep reading and revising until you are confident your text reflects your thoughts and addresses the principal issues most effectively.

5.1.2 Make Fewer Words Do More Work Through Tight-Construction

As advised by Strunk and White:

> Vigorous writing is concise. A sentence should contain no unnecessary words, a paragraph no unnecessary sentences, for the same reason that a drawing should have no unnecessary lines and a machine no unnecessary parts This requires not that the writer make all sentences short, or avoid all detail and treat subjects only in outline, but that every word tell.[3]

So how do you get there? Slowly and deliberately. When crunching your content to tighten your text, start with the large issues first. Ask yourself: **(1)** Do my words flow? **(2)** Is there an overall sense of moving forward? **(3)** Is there a feeling of continuity and coherence? **(4)** If not, do I need to move a sentence? **(5)** Have I been attentive to the length of my sentences? **(6)** Have I created a linkage between paragraphs? **(7)** Have I unnecessarily digressed to reinforce a position that was already sufficiently addressed?

Careful revisions need not be tedious, but they generally take time, requiring your best effort at objectivity. The mindset is akin to a lyricist trying to match her words to the melody. There will be portions where the needed change is readily apparent; other times, you may have to play and replay the music in your head until every word fits where it belongs. Or, as English satirist Jonathan Swift said, "proper words in proper places."

Then, move on to the smaller, gritty issues. Are you building sturdy fences? A sentence is finished only when the order of the words cannot be revised without harming its thought or offending the reader's eye. Count the syllables in your words, count the words in each sentence, and count the number of words in a paragraph. Look for fat. Then trim it. Check on the rhythm of your sentences. Check on the consistency of tenses, syntax and diction. Your choice of words makes all the difference in creating an effective writing style. A key guideline is to use strong, simple concrete nouns and verbs with no more modifiers than necessary to convey your thought on an issue. It all begins with patience, diligence and self-discipline, and evolves into a habit; a habit that will serve you well.

Finally, be ever mindful of the reader's eye. In addition to your content, form matters. Ancient writings, whether on stone, papyrus or parchment, began with the initial word on the first line and continued breathlessly to the bottom of the page, with nary a break. Eventually, some chronicler(s) thought of the reader's eye. Then, in different times and countries, ancient texts began including needed breaks between the thoughts expressed by the writer. This keen observation led to more space between words and sentences and, ultimately, the creation of paragraphs and chapters. *Don't write like the ancients.* The form in which you deliver written words matters. Writing dominated by multi-syllable words, long sentences and paragraphs, the absence of headings and very little blank space on the page is a surefire turnoff. Be mindful of form as well as content. It matters greatly.

5.1.3 Be Positive & Direct

Your sentences should assert a position, proclaim a thought or express a proposition. No matter how mundane, all your pronouncements should declare cogent thoughts. Even a negative thought should be expressed in a positive form. It's easier to understand what is than what is not. As said elsewhere in this text, "You win your case by making your case."

Following are some examples:

Original: The facts relied upon by plaintiff appear to provide no support that it was this defendant who is responsible for his losses.

Edited: Plaintiff's pleadings contain no facts showing that this defendant caused his losses.

Original: The scientific expert will, at the time of trial, be called as a witness by the defense counsel.

Edited: At trial, defendant will call her scientific expert as a witness.

5.1.4 Be Specific

You will never get to clarity by relying upon vague vocabulary. The best legal writing aims to highlight the key details in simple terms. Precise, concrete, vivid language is superior because it saves your reader from having to translate words into thought. Vague terms, abstract nouns and nominalizations (see Chapter Two) have the potential to "squeeze the life out of sentences."[4]

Following are some examples:

Original: The contract contains numerous provisions, the language of which creates confusion because they conflict with the parties stated purpose in the preamble to the agreement.

Edited: Multiple provisions in the contract conflict with the agreement's preamble, creating confusion.

Original: The daily actions of the defendant employer toward his female employees had created a workplace environment that was downright hostile.

Edited: Defendant's conduct created a hostile work environment for his female employees.

5.1.5 Use the Active Voice; Avoid the Passive Voice

Vigor in your prose is essential. If you want your reader to keep reading, you must speak with an assertive voice. You achieve that through active verbs. Verbs make things happen. They build muscle. They generate energy. If your sentences seem to sag or lack dynamism, blame the verbs *or* the lack thereof. If your sentences zing home your message with meaning, credit the verbs. "Nurture the verb as though the life of your sentence depended upon it."[5] Effective writers must develop the mindset to prefer the active voice. It is more plainspoken and its meaning is clearer. It infuses your writing with more authority and directness to your readers. "Just as English tends to move straight ahead from subject to verb to object, it also works best when it goes straight to the point."[6] Avoid the passive voice like a deadly virus.

You can recognize passive-voice expressions because the verb phrase usually includes a form of be, such as *am, is, was, were, are* or *been*. In a passive sentence, the person or thing doing the action (the actor) is usually preceded by the word "by." Active sentences generally are in the form of "A did B." Passive sentences, however, are in the form of "B was done to A." Accordingly, active sentences are easier to read. The passive voice "robs sentences of energy, adds unnecessary words, seeds a slew of wretched participles and prepositions, and leaves questions unanswered... Vigorous, clear, and concise writing demands sentences with muscle, strong active verbs cast in the active voice."[7]

Following are some examples:

Original: What would have been a disaster, was averted by the quick thinking of defendant.

Edited: Defendant's quick thinking prevented a disaster.

Original: The injuries sustained by plaintiff were not a result of anyone's negligence.

Edited: Plaintiff's injuries were free of negligence.

5.1.6 Effective Style is Lucid & Potent

It's not the job of your reader to sort through a word salad and figure out your message. It's your job to make yourself understood. Whether termed lucidity, intelligibility or clarity of expression, it is essential that attorneys be able to make themselves understood at all times, in all circumstances, to all readers and all listeners. Always.

Failure to clearly express your client's position is unacceptable. Any time an attorney delivers a stumbling, bumbling, half-witted message it reflects poorly upon our entire profession. As Lincoln said, "Better to remain silent and be thought a fool than to speak out and remove all doubt." If you can't deliver a clear, well-reasoned message, then remain silent. This handbook illustrates multiple ways to ensure your message is readily understood and prevent ambiguity. You must be mindful of everything from syntax, diction and rhythm to linking, coherence and punctuation. Mastering those details will aid you in making your message lucid.

Yet, the potency of your message is another matter. At times, the power of your message is limited by the law supporting your position. Sometimes in our profession, it's about cutting your losses rather than securing a victory. Other times, it's about asking your reader, whether a client, colleague or the court, to consider the value of a novel approach to a problem. You may also be confronted with a legal standard that requires a new look as a result of changes in society. Even with bad facts and lousy law, you can still deliver a forceful message. Concede your weaknesses and highlight your strengths. Raise thorny questions and offer novel solutions. Utilizing the appropriate tools, there may be times when candor, lucidity and a thoughtful discussion of both the facts and law become your potency. Never underestimate the forcefulness of unrestrained plain-spokenness and common-sense solutions, even if the solution entails compromise. Sometimes, creativity is the answer to a problem for which existing legal standards provide only limited guidance.

5.1.7 Go Lightly on Modifiers

Adjectives modify nouns and are often called "describing words" because they give us details about a noun, such *as what it looks like* (the blue car), *how many* there are (the seven children) or *which one* it is (the last building on the street). Adverbs modify or describe a verb, adjective or another adverb, adding information to the sentence. Scrutinize your sentences as if you were cross-examining a witness. Is that adjective essential to define the subject of your sentence, or is it there as an ornament? Adverbs modifying verbs and adjectives have the excuse that they tell us *why, where, when* and *how*, but frequently they clutter sentences. It's rare that the length of your first draft cannot be shortened by simply examining your modifiers.

Following are some examples:

Original: The large, gray slabs of concrete violently destroyed every single, solitary thing in their path as they collapsed totally on their way to the ground, sparing nothing in their path, creating an enormous pile of rubble.

Edited: As they collapsed, the concrete slabs destroyed everything in their path, creating a pile of rubble.

Original: The review and oversight role of the FDA with regard to the development, manufacture and marketing of new prescription medications is a costly and time-consuming process, generally misunderstood by the public.

Edited: FDA's role in the approval of new prescription medications is a cumbersome process, rarely explained to the public.

Always ask, is that adjective necessary? What does that adverb add to the potency of this or that verb or adjective? Bestselling author, Stephen King once wrote, "I believe the road to hell is paved with adverbs."[8] Or, to quote Harper Lee speaking through Scout, "Atticus told me to delete the adjectives and I'd have the facts."[9] More often than not, strong nouns and strong verbs don't need to be modified, highlighted or accentuated. They stand on their own.

5.2 Misplaced Words & Phrases

5.2.1 Misplaced Modifiers

Misplaced modifiers are words or phrases that are improperly separated from the word it modifies or describes. Because of the separation, sentences with this error often read/sound awkward or confusing. Misplaced modifiers can usually be corrected by moving the modifier to a more logical place in the sentence, generally next to the word it modifies. Misplaced adjectives, adverbs or modifying phrases can all hamper the flow of your style. To avoid ambiguity, the subject of a sentence and the principal verb shouldn't be unnecessarily separated by modifying words or phrases.

Following are some examples:

• All the jurors were not present.

versus

Not all the jurors were present.

• Words spoken heatedly before a jury is never wise.

versus

It is never wise to speak heatedly before a jury.

- Having thrown a book at the lawyer the day before, the judge ordered the sheriff to stand next to Mr. Brown.

versus

Because Mr. Brown threw a book the day before, the judge ordered the sheriff to stand next to him.

5.2.2 Dangling Participles

A participle is a verb that functions as an adjective. Present participles end in *ing*. They are verbs that describe a continuous action, e.g., writing, talking, listening, etc. A participle phrase is a group of words, containing a participle, that modifies the subject of a sentence. When a participle phrase "dangles" the modifier is out of place, or too far away from the subject, resulting in confusion for the reader.

Following are some examples:

- While leaving the courthouse, the judge saw the jurors as she was standing at her desk and looking out her window.

versus

While standing at her desk and looking out her window, the judge saw the jurors leaving the courthouse.

- Preparing a memo following the close of testimony, the lawyer was typing his notes to his client.

versus

Typing his notes following the close of testimony, the lawyer was preparing a memo to his client.

5.2.3 Split infinitives

Dictionary definitions of the word *infinitive* can become involved, thus, for our discussion, the infinitive is the form of the verb that has *to* in front of it: *to talk, to write, to listen.* Infinitives never function in sentences as verbs but rather as adverbs, adjectives or nouns. To split an infinitive is to put a word or words between the infinitive marker—the word *to*—and the root verb that follows it. A common example used by Strunk and White is the *Star Trek* phrase "to boldly go." Here, the infinitive *to go* is split by the adverb *boldly.* As discussed earlier, today's English language evolved out of an effort to accommodate the Britons, the French, and the Church during the Middle Ages. The oft-repeated theory is that the rule against splitting an infinitive is a product of the effort to make English grammar function the way Latin grammar does. In Latin, an infinitive is a single word and, as a result, cannot be split. Regardless of its source, this "rule" has caused much discussion between those who value adherence to tradition and those who value clarity and readability above all else. Truth be told, people regularly split their infinitives. It's the rare judge, client or colleague who will take you to task for splitting an infinitive.

5.3 Punctuation

Used correctly, punctuation can guide your readers smoothly through your sentences and paragraphs, from one thought to another. Misused, it can do the opposite. Proper punctuation is a critical component of an effective style. Repeated mistakes with punctuation undermine your credibility with the reader.

Relying heavily upon the guidance rendered by Strunk and White and the OED, what follows is a concise discussion of the 15 primary tools of punctuation.

1. **Comma**: In a series of three or more terms with a single conjunction, use a comma after each term except the last. Enclose parenthetic expressions between commas. Place a comma before a conjunction introducing an independent clause. Do not join independent clauses with a comma; the proper punctuation is a semicolon.

2. **Semicolon:** Its primary role is to mark a break stronger than a comma but not as final as a period. It is used between two main clauses that balance each other and are too closely linked to be made into separate sentences. Semicolons are also used as a stronger division in a sentence that already contains commas, and are used to separate more than individual words, but phrases.

3. **Colon**: There are three main uses: **(1)** between two main clauses in cases where the second clause explains or follows from the first, **(2)** to introduce a list or **(3)** before a quotation.

4. **Period**; It is used primarily to mark the end of a sentence that is a complete statement and with abbreviations and website addresses.

5. **Quotation marks**: They are used when you are quoting a passage of 50 or fewer words (when more than 50 set off the quote) and when you are referring to a word or phrase, followed by an explanation or definition.

6. **Italics**: This tool is used primarily for emphasis or contrast, namely, to draw *attention* to a term or portion of your text.

7. **Parentheses**: Typically, they are used to set off a strong or weak interruption, much like a pair of dashes or a pair of bracketing commas.

8. **Brackets**: They are mainly used to enclose words added by someone other than the original writer or speaker, typically in order to clarify the situation.

9. **Dash**: A dash is a mark of separation stronger than a comma, less formal than a colon, and more relaxed than parentheses. Do not overuse dashes.

10. **Hyphen**: When two or more words are combined to form a compound adjective, a hyphen is usually required.

11. **Apostrophe**: It is used for both contractions (appearing in the place of letters) and to show possession, with the word (or name) spelled with 's at the end.

12. **Ellipses**: The use of dots ... to show the omission of words that are unnecessary in a quote.

13. **Slash**: It has several uses, all rather minor. The most common examples are to separate alternatives, abbreviations and fractions.

14. **Question mark**: It is placed at the end of a sentence that is a direct question. It is not used with an indirect question.

15. **Exclamation point**: Known informally as a *bang* or a *shriek*, it is used at the end of a sentence or a short phrase that expresses very strong feeling. It's rare that an exclamation point adds to a lawyer's style.

Part Three

PREPARATION OF NON-LITIGATION DOCUMENTS

The lawyer's greatest weapon is clarity,
and its whetstone is succinctness.

—Judge E.B. Prettyman

Chapter Six

A PRIMER ON DRAFTING CONTRACTS

Contents

6.1 Know Your Deal

Clients request lawyers to secure their relationships with others by drafting contracts in countless situations; everything from leases, easements and sales of real estate, to matrimonial settlements, corporate bylaws and partnerships. This chapter will not address the many circumstances in which an agreement is essential;[1] rather, the aim is to highlight the basic principles of drafting contracts to aid lawyers when acting as the scrivener of a contract, regardless of the situation.

Serving as a scrivener can be a challenge to one's writing skills. Observed through a wide-angle lens, the act of drafting contracts is usually seen as part of a larger planning process aimed at solidifying a client's position prior to proceeding with a new venture. Preparing an agreement of any significance is essentially a zero-based effort. Contracts should be constructed paragraph by paragraph, with a reason for including every provision, *nay* every word. Regardless of how many agreements a lawyer may have previously prepared in similar situations, she should assume nothing. New parties, at a different point in time, bring wrinkles unique to a client's situation. Those wrinkles must be addressed individually. With contracts, as with nearly everything lawyers do, "know your deal" applies with equal force, namely, the need to ask questions, investigate all the pertinent facts and become oriented to your client's needs, wants and expectations.

One of the more challenging aspects of practicing law is managing other people's expectations. In drafting an agreement, a clear understanding of the parties' expectations is a necessity. That process begins with a thorough interview of your client (whether *via* conversation or written answers to a questionnaire), together with available input from the other party. You must address everything, including: *Who is ...? What is...? When is...? What is the consideration? What are the obligations? What are the consequences of failing to perform?* Experienced attorneys know to keep checklists of questions for various types of contracts when reviewing a client's need for an agreement, continually refining those checklists. Prior to preparing the initial draft of your client's agreement, every effort should be made to confirm that the parties to the undertaking are moving forward in unison. Failure to do so can lead to unhappy clients and headaches for lawyers. To avoid this, once you've gathered all available information, prepare a numbered-paragraph memorandum summarizing your understanding of the deal. Share your memorandum with your client, and upon receipt of his approval, submit the memo or draft agreement to counsel for the other parties.

Drafting contracts is not about seeking out forms found in legal treatises or online, but rather entails the responsibility of accurately expressing the understanding of the parties to an agreement. When the opportunity presents itself, you should seek to prepare the first draft. Generally, most of the language contained in the initial draft finds its way into the final draft. Should you be presented with a draft agreement by the other party's attorney, do not prepare a new draft in response (unless it's *godawful*); simply comment on any suggested changes, referencing those paragraphs in need of modification. Each time you begin the process of preparing a contract for a transaction of any consequence, it is vital that you have the proper mindset of a scrivener.

Contracts are consequential private legislation. When you draft the terms of a negotiated, arms-length agreement, you are establishing the standards, control mechanisms and potential penalties that will bind, guide and constrain the parties. You are writing "the law" that provides for the anticipated benefits flowing from the parties' ventures, together with possible liabilities should the enterprise incur difficulties or should either party fail to comply with the terms of the agreement. The document you prepare will state the consideration, namely, promises of performance by the parties, and set down the parameters of the miniature world they hope to create for themselves. You must also be mindful of the real-world context in which the agreement will be enforced. For that reason, always research the relevant law.

To some extent, every contract requires researching the law to ensure you are not overlooking any pertinent standards that should be referenced in the agreement. You must be attuned to the relevant statutes, judicial decisions or administrative regulations that may impact upon the miniature world being created by your client. In addition to examining the external law, inquire of your client as to the industry standards, practices and customs peculiar to the transaction. The interview of your client should aid you in understanding not just her goals but also, the context in which the parties will be operating. The reason for having solid footing in the applicable law is that until given a reason to the contrary, third parties reviewing the contract terms are obliged to respect your chosen language. This is especially true of the court system, which "never interferes until a promise has been broken."[2] And when our courts become involved, they rely upon the plain meaning of your words, seeking only to enforce that language. Therefore, it is essential that you correctly articulate the meeting of the minds between the parties, consistent with any applicable legal standards. That is your responsibility as a scrivener.

6.2 Clarity & Flexibility

Like all legal writing, contract language must be precise and concise, yet it must also be flexible, capable of adapting to a relationship that may evolve. Why? Because contracts "are plans for a future full of circumstances that neither the drafter nor the client can presently know about...The most useful language to accomplish flexibility is often vague rather than precise, general rather than particular."[3] By using language that increases a document's flexibility, the parties are empowered to interpret those provisions within the context of any changed circumstances.

Below are three hypothetical contractual relationships. Each illustrates some of the issues to which a lawyer must be attentive when drafting a comprehensive agreement integral to the parties' success: **(1)** lease of a restaurant, **(2)** sale of a bus company and **(3)** construction of a new "green" office building. The parties to these transactions have limited vision into the future, thus it is important that their agreement be sufficiently flexible to enable them to work through problems if/when they arise. (Note: the issues, concerns and questions raised here are not exhaustive. The points needed to be addressed may be far more involved in the real world.)

Lease of a Restaurant: Your client wishes to lease an existing restaurant that appears lucrative. The owner/landlord is confident your client will prosper and has proposed a below-market-rate lease with a percentage rent add-on. Despite a recent makeover of the restaurant, there are several concerns: age of the building, its plumbing and HVAC systems, and kitchen equipment. What follows are some of the questions best addressed through language that permits flexibility.

- **Rent**: Below-market-rate lease payment, plus, percentage rent raises these questions: Will there be cost-of-living increases on the base rent? Regarding percentage rent, is the existing method of bookkeeping acceptable to the tenant? How often may the restaurant's books be examined by the landlord? What occurs if there is a dispute over the restaurant's revenue under your client's management? Will the tenant have the option to renew? If so, what is the time frame for delivering notice to the landlord?

- **Repairs**: How will the lease address repairs? Tenant needs certainty as to who makes repairs to what item of equipment, so what are the best means to avoid uncertainty? With regards to critical systems, should the newer systems be the responsibility of the landlord, and the older systems the responsibility of the tenant, or the reverse?

- **Replacement of Essential Equipment**: Under what circumstances, will equipment no longer under warranty be the responsibility of the landlord? In the event there is a dispute, should either party have the right to proceed with repairs subject to a reservation of rights to seek reimbursement? Should disputes be resolved *via* binding arbitration or another means? Under what circumstances would the losing party be responsible for counsel fees?

Sale of a Bus Company: Your client is purchasing an operating business and acquiring its current assets and liabilities. A key asset is several large tourism-related contracts that provide a significant portion of the bus company's revenue. Loss of any of these contracts would create major problems. The CEO of the bus company has agreed to hold a mortgage to finance the sale to your client. What follows are some of the questions best addressed through language that permits flexibility.

- **Debts and Licenses**: How do the parties address the multiple liens against the conveyed property, both real estate and equipment? If a debt holder declines to accept the buyer as the new guarantor, will the seller reaffirm those debts? How will the parties address obstacles that delay the timely transfer of the various licenses required for the bus company? Should there be outstanding debts exceeding those calculated at the time of closing on the sale, how will they be addressed? Will unilateral offset of mortgage payments be permitted?

- **Key Personnel**: The bus company is overseen by a longtime manager; both parties want him to remain in his position until all debts owed by the buyer to the seller are satisfied. What is the best means to secure this arrangement? To address the possibility of the manager's untimely demise, will the buyer be permitted to purchase insurance on the manager's life? Should the manager die unexpectedly, how will the insurance proceeds be divided? How will a new manager be chosen if the manager dies or retires?

- **Key Customers**: The loss of any of the tourism-related contracts would severely impact the value of the company and its revenue stream. Assuming no fault of the buyer, how should such a potential loss be addressed? What would be a reasonable adjustment to the amount of future mortgage payments by the buyer to the seller? Is it possible to arrive at a pre-determined formula?

Construction of a New "Green" Office Building: Your client has decided to build an office building that will be "green" in its design, materials and construction. Environmental sustainability is a core feature of the client's plans, as well as the ability to adapt to changing circumstances. What follows are some of the questions best addressed through language that permits flexibility.

- **Green Standards**: What/who will be the final authority (published studies, and/or agreed-upon expert(s)) on what are the most energy-efficient materials? Can either party suggest *greener* redesign(s) when feasible and cost effective? In the event of a disagreement, how will issues be resolved?

- **Escalation Clause on Pricing**: Supply and potential increased costs of the needed energy-efficient materials can become an issue. Price escalation questions: **(1)** Can the contractor definitively identify those construction materials that may be subject to price escalation? **(2)** Is there a reasonable means for calculating any increased costs necessitated by the substitution of materials? **(3)** What are the best means to assure the owner that the contractor has used his best efforts to prevent a price escalation?

- **Method for Dispute Resolution**: Disputes must not delay construction. Should either party reject the other side's opinion on what are the most energy-efficient materials or costs involved, how do they efficiently resolve their dispute? Mediation? Binding arbitration? Litigation, with both parties reserving their rights while construction proceeds?

Finally, drafting contracts requires a different mindset than drafting pleadings. To achieve a document that is sufficiently pliable to remain relevant in the years ahead, it may be necessary to write some provisions in generalities—excluding unlikely occurrences—rather than with exactness, and on other issues, to utilize a vague vocabulary rather than explicit wording. Where appropriate, such an approach ensures a document that can adapt to the parties' relationsTerms and phrases providing flexibility are limited only by a lawyer's creativity. Examples follow: **(1)** in accord with industry practice; **(2)** as routinely contemplated in the business community of this locale; **(3)** within a reasonable time under all the circumstances; **(4)** as permitted by customary practices in (type of) business; **(5)** on terms and conditions generally acceptable by like business people in the greater (city) metropolitan region; **(6)** when compared to the action of reasonable business people in the same or similar circumstances, and **(7)** as could be reasonably anticipated in the workplace of (type of) businesses of this locale. By utilizing such language, you are sanctioning reasonable interpretations suited for new circumstances in the future. Should a dispute arise, the parties are, to a large extent, bound by the "reasonable person" standard you have built into the agreement.

As the scrivener, your aim is to draft an agreement that affords sufficient pliability by enabling/compelling the parties to resolve their differences as their relationship evolves. Serious disputes may require independent arbiters to suggest solutions, or the retention of expert opinions. Ideally, your contract language should be pliable enough to facilitate the resolution of disputes, rather than being so confining that it unconsciously fosters confrontations.

6.3 Table of Contents & Preamble

Creating a table of contents is helpful in orienting a first-time reader of your contract. Your aim is to convince the reader she is in the hands of a capable, well-organized attorney. As presented in each chapter in this handbook, a quick list located at the beginning of your document will aid the reader's eye in navigating the agreement's terms. Appearing on the first page, immediately preceding the preamble, the scrivener should create a list of the primary provisions and subparts of the contract, together with their page numbers. Typically, the table of con-

tents together with the definitions will be the final portion of
the document you prepare once you have finalized the headings
(and page numbers) to be used in presenting the contract's various provisions.

It's helpful to always begin a contract with a preamble. The
preamble to an agreement is similar to a preliminary statement
of a brief filed with the court. As discussed in Chapter Three
regarding the preparation of your "lead," and in Chapter Nine
on preliminary statements, your preamble must tell readers of
the agreement the *who*, the *what*, the *why* and the *how* of the
undertaking the parties wish to pursue together, and *where* they
plan to go with it, subject to the benefits and burdens detailed
in later provisions. Your preamble must concisely recite the status of the parties and express the goals for their venture. Simply
state what the deal is all about. Give yourself a word budget of
200–350 words; if you think you need more words, maybe you
don't understand your deal as well as you should.

Example of Preamble for an LLC

Suzanne Thompson ("Sue") and Frederick Connors
("Fred) wish to create a consulting firm whose target
clients are casino hotels engaging in sports betting.
Sue's personality and past employment qualify her to
lead the new firm's marketing efforts, soliciting casino CEOs. Sue has sufficient knowledge of sports betting to be conversant with prospective clients. Fred
has worked in the information technology field for the
past 25 years. He is also an avid sports fan. Over the
years, Fred has done well gambling on sporting events.
Fred has developed software for a new "app" that enables casinos to track their customers' betting habits

and provide them with up-to-date information on the teams and athletes in whom they are most interested. As planned, the new firm's revenue will be a percentage of the wagers made by customers identified by the firm for the casinos.

Sue and Fred have each invested $150,000, for a total of $300,000, to hire staff, rent space and outfit the leased premises. Sue will be the CEO and Fred the COO. Their duties are described herein. The parties anticipate limited income during the initial six months of operations, with prospects of $1,000,000 in revenue by the end of the first 18 months. In the event the firm fails to generate a minimum of $500,000 after 18 months, each party will invest an additional $50,000. Finally, should the firm fail to generate a minimum of $1,500,000 within 36 months of the date of this agreement, Sue and Fred shall confer on the potential dissolution of their firm.

6.4 Provide for the Downside

As stated by the legendary Justice Oliver Wendell Holmes, "It is true that, when people make contracts, they usually contemplate the performance rather than the breach."[4] As defined by the Restatement of Contracts, "A breach of contract is a non-performance of any contractual duty of immediate performance. A breach may be total or partial, and may take place by failure to perform acts promised, by prevention or hindrance, or by repudiation."[5] In order for a claimant to be successful, "A plaintiff bringing a cause of action for breach of contract must establish: **(1)** the existence of a valid contract with plaintiff and defendant; **(2)** a breach of the contract by defendant; **(3)** performance by the plaintiff of his/her obligations under the contract; and **(4)** resulting damages."[6]

Contractual relationships fail for a variety of reasons. Scriveners must provide for the errant party who violates the agreement's terms or fails to perform as originally contemplated. You must address how to resolve disputes. Mediation? Arbitration? Litigation? The three contracts discussed above in Section 6.2 provide multiple examples of how things can go wrong. In the restaurant lease a dispute over the percentage rent is foreseeable; an independent and respected accounting firm could be designated as the initial means to resolve disputes. In the sale of a bus company, the loss of a key customer could be catastrophic; assuming no fault of the buyer, provisions might provide for rescission of the contract, to be overseen by an arbiter mutually acceptable to the parties. With the construction of a new "green" office building, availability of the needed materials might become a threat to a timely completion; provisions for acceptable back-up suppliers and/or materials must be recited.

In all three situations, with regard to the consequences of either party's failure to perform as agreed, the scrivener should consider the following: **(1)** how to resolve disputes; **(2)** possible penalties, namely money damages, and/or prescriptive measures and **(3)** when feasible, ability of the non-breaching party to continue with the venture.

Finally, there is the need to consider language/phraseology that creates what many lawyers refer to as an "integrated contract." When a contract contains language essentially stating *this contract represents the entire understanding between the parties*, it becomes an integrated contract. An integrated contract bars the admission of evidence of understandings reached prior to the contract's execution—having the potential to vary its terms—but not reflected in a writing by the parties. It is wise to include such language in most contracts.

6.5 Define Key Terms

Definitions are essential and the language used can expand or constrain flexibility. Yet definitions are best left until all other contract provisions are established. Then, review the key terms that require defining based upon their complexity, pivotal role or frequent recital in the contract. There can be no misunderstanding as to **(1)** who is responsible for doing what, **(2)** the planned results of the parties' venture and **(3)** the consequences to any party who fails to perform. Whether acquiring real property (block and lot number) sale of business interests (tax ID numbers) or an agreement to provide personal services (resume` of the individual retained), etc., the key terms upon which the relationship rests must be defined with contextual clarity. Though generally drafted last, definitions should appear in the agreement following the preamble.

What follows are seven questions you should consider when composing definitions:

1. Do you rely upon plain language and try your best to minimize the use of jargon in defining terms?

2. Do you utilize a tool such as quotation marks or all capital letters to highlight defined terms so readers know the term has a specific definition?

3. Do you state the definition for a given term the first time it appears in the contract, or limit recital of definitions to the definition section only?

4. Do you include references to statutes or regulations, or omit them for inclusion in a separate section of the contract?

5. Do you use each defined term throughout the agreement in a manner consistent with your stated definitions?

6. Do you list the definitions alphabetically, or rank them in importance, or recite them based upon the frequency with which they appear in the contract?

7. Do you want as many definitions as possible, or as few as are necessary? (Depending upon the circumstances, either preference may impact upon overall flexibility.)

Utilizing the three hypothetical contracts discussed in Section 6.2 of this handbook, what follows is a partial list of examples of those terms that ought to be defined.

Restaurant Lease: **(1)** essential systems named and described in addendum; **(2)** essential equipment described, with serial number, etc. in an addendum; **(3)** vendors named with details in an addendum; **(4)** key employees named, with salaries and duties detailed in an addendum; **(5)** liquor license: identify by license number and date of issuance, discuss transfer in body of lease

Bus Company: **(1)** real property defined by block and lot on tax map; **(2)** equipment defined by serial number, manufacturer and model; **(3)** outstanding liabilities recited and detailed in an addendum; **(4)** licenses identified by issuing agency and expiration date; **(5)** key contracts by name of client and expiration date, plus previous year's income

<u>Green Building</u>: **(1)** construction documents defined by name of architect, AIA license number and project number; **(2)** acknowledged authorities (publications, regulations or experts) on "green" construction materials; **(3)** project manager and his authority as the owner's inspector; **(4)** identity of expert(s) and/or mediator(s) to assist in resolution of disputes; **(5)** liquidated damages, how they are calculated and the basis for the same

6.6 Readability

As you go forward in addressing the pertinent issues in drafting an agreement, "readability" is a top priority. A fundamental rule of effective writing is that good organization enhances understandability. *Form* influences a reader's ability to absorb *substance*. Three guideposts will aid your efforts to create a readable contract.

(1) Headings and subheadings using bold print, capital letters and Arabic and/or Roman numerals to delineate provisions, will help lead the reader's eye through the document; each enables retention of the content. Simple headings—underlined, in capital letters or bold print—will provide meaningful information about the content of each provision and signal divisions in the material. Your aim is not only to eliminate dense prose but also to avoid content that looks dense. To that end, white space is easier on the reader's eye. Whether paper or electronic, consider these guidelines for each page: **(a)** consistent borders, top and bottom, ditto as to side margins (i.e., blank space equaling 33 percent to 40 percent); **(b)** a minimum of one or two paragraph breaks per page; and **(c)** the first line of each paragraph indented, content double-spaced.

(2) As discussed in Chapter Two, avoid jargon and legalisms. Use simple words. Of necessity, there may be various statutes, regulations or possibly controlling case law that must be cited. When you refer to legal standards provide an explanation of one to three short sentences where necessary to prevent confusion over the meaning or importance of the term and its impact upon the parties' relationship. When the legal context of the transaction is pivotal to its success, address the limits created by the law in sufficient detail to avoid doubt as to the relevant legal standards and their influence over the parties' relationship.

(3) Short sentences and minimal paragraphs of three to seven sentences (150–200 words) should be used for individual provisions, using a type and font size that is easy on the reader's eye, akin to the font on this page. Lawyers have differing opinions on the fonts they prefer and which type of right-hand margin is easier on the reader's eye, a justified margin or a ragged right-hand margin. Either one will work.

This text is justified, but on a document greater than ten pages, counsel may want to do as many print newspapers do, utilize both a justified and ragged right margin for alternate pages or sections of the contract. After finalizing the language, you may need to prepare several drafts of the final form. Stay at it. With readability by a stranger in mind (particularly the client), you will create a reader-friendly *form* that eases the absorption and retention of the *substance*.

Chapter Seven

EMAIL, LETTERS, MEMOS & EDITING

❖●❖

Aside from pleadings (Chapter Eight) and briefs (Chapter Nine), as a professional writer in the law, there are essentially three types of written communications in your law practice: **(1)** email, **(2)** letters and **(3)** memos. Because most of your communications with others are confined to a digital format, particularly email, there is, unfortunately, a potential to treat digital messages with less care than those in "hard copy" paper format. One consequence of digital messages is the tendency not to worry about typos, grammatical errors and run-on sentences. Do not become careless in *any* written interactions. Whether digital or hard copy, today nearly everything lawyers write is saved in some type of digital format. Though digital documents can be deleted or lost, with information technology (IT) experts they are often recoverable. Re-read everything—and, as needed, edit and revise—before hitting the "send" button. Regardless of the format, an email, a letter, or a memo, each requires research, organization and clarity of expression. Aligning the means of your communication to your intentions for the message usually controls the choice made. Generally, emails are for internal or external communications, letters are for external communications, and memos are for internal communications.

7.1 Email

In the pre-Internet era, it was common for an attorney to receive a letter from a client or colleague, consider the message, perhaps research the issue raised, and then compose a thoughtful response. Such tasks could take hours, the effort sometimes spanning days. Today, what once was routine is rare. Clients, adversaries, and even the courts increasingly expect prompt replies from you. In the past, a delay in replying provided a lawyer with the opportunity for careful deliberation. For many people, that's no longer acceptable. Immediate answers are expected. In today's law firms, email is the dominant means of communication. Careless errors can leave a negative impression. Responsible use of email requires a deliberate and thoughtful approach. What follows are six suggestions a/k/a "rules" for use of email that practicing attorneys should consider making part of their routine.

Know Your Audience: Rule 1 in every communication is "know your audience." The considerations regarding your audience are basically three: **(a)** To whom is your email written and what (if anything) are you hoping to learn from the recipients? **(b)** In addition to your primary recipient, is there anyone else interested in the content of the message? **(c)** Is anyone being openly copied or blind copied?

As you sit before the keyboard, give thoughtful attention to your audience, who they should be, and what you want from them. Depending upon their interests and/or status, separate emails may be necessary. Finally, do not fill in your intended recipients until you have composed and proofread the entire content of your message. A hasty stroke of the "Send" button, resulting in unintended recipients, can prove embarrassing.

What is Your Objective and/or Subject: Email should be used warily. Many of your thoughts on issues arising in your law practice are best expressed by a telephone call or still better, when within your law firm, by a brief face-to-face conversation. When an exchange of ideas or issues among law firm colleagues in search of a solution is appropriate, email is probably not the best means. Often, when the communications are among members of the same law firm regarding a challenging issue, the collective time invested in having a brief in-person meeting may be less than back-and-forth messaging via email.

Also, what is the subject you wish to pursue? Email is best utilized for a brief communication of objective facts, the raising of a question(s), or furnishing a short answer(s). Such emails may entail: documenting events; confirming a meeting or a set of circumstances; replying to a discussion; or transmitting information, inclusive of data or documents, or some similar information. Excessive use of email can lead to the wrong subjects being included in emails. Email works best when your subjects are routine matters.

Be Mindful of Your Tone: Your tone must always be polite and professional. Workplace studies show that it can be difficult for the sender to establish the correct tone in an email.

Yet, the ability of the recipient to interpret tone is even harder. According to the American Psychological Association, people sending an email frequently overestimated a recipient's ability to identify whether an email's tone was serious or sarcastic. The senders wrongly believed 80 percent of the recipients would get it right, when roughly 56 percent did.[1] Thus, it's critical that you think carefully about the words you use and how you frame your email. When you have finished your first draft, pause to reflect on how your words might be interpreted (or misinterpreted) by the recipient.

In terms of setting your tone, proceed carefully. You can never duplicate in-person communications. One-to-one, thoughtful discussions between lawyers are significantly enabled by facial gestures, voice intonation and the easy exchange of thoughts supported by documents. That is not possible with email. Thus, every effort should be made to set the tone in your initial sentence. Using qualifying language, it is possible to minimize the chances of a message being misinterpreted. Generally, sensitive matters should not be addressed via email. As a member of the bar, other than close staff, friends and families, *all* of your communications must have a professional tone. Twelve examples of how to set the tone of your message in the first sentence are provided in Chapter Four. Yet even they should be used cautiously, mindful of the recipients and what you wish to convey and hope to learn from them.

Be Mindful of the Subject or "Re" Line: When it comes to clarity of messaging, the subject line ought to function as a book or chapter title, announcing what is to follow. Upon reading the subject line, the reader should have no doubt about **(a)** the subject, **(b)** the purpose of the email, and **(c)** hopefully, the need to read the email. For example, a subject line that reads "Litigation Memo" is so general that it provides little-to-no guidance. Yet if that same line read "MEMO: Discussion of Petition for Injunctive Relief," your reader will know why to continue reading. Other helpful information in the subject line might include the security designation, a reply-by date, and any other details that aids in the future retrieval of your email.

Think Through Your Message and Proofread Every Email: Be precise and concise. Get to the point of the communication in the opening line or paragraph. Your message must be unmistakably clear in its content, leaving nothing capable of being misconstrued by the recipient. Be as careful in your syntax, diction, grammar and punctuation as you would in any formal legal writing. If several related subjects can be combined into a single email via numbered paragraphs, that is generally preferable to multiple emails, unless the length of your message makes a single memo more coherent. Also, be mindful of the recommended word budget for emails of 200–250 words; if you need more words, consider writing a short memo and sending it as an attachment. Then save your memo to the appropriate file. *Always* proofread for both accuracy and clarity of content. That goes beyond typos and includes the length and quality of the email. Time spent on proofreading will contribute not only to effective communication but also to the task described and the results sought in the email itself. Additionally, be careful to confirm the recipients; "Auto-Fill" can be a source of embarrassing errors in listing the wrong recipients.

Finally, with regard to a lengthy email versus a short memo, consider preparing a draft document on a separate clean page of your computer screen. Then, after you have proofread and edited it, assess its overall importance. Is it just another email that can be copied and pasted into your email account, or is it a document of particular importance that ought to be in the form of a letter, email or attachment as a memorandum? The form may facilitate prompt retrieval in the future.

Be Mindful of Security: Emails are easily shared at the stroke of a key without the original sender's knowledge; thus, you never know with whom your email may be shared. If the subject is personal, private, or confidential—each having its own level of security—it should be so indicated. Likewise, if a "read-receipt" is needed, be sure to so mark the email. That said, such designations cannot be relied upon with confidence. With regard to confidential information, think through the situation and purposefully decide what should be included in or attached to an email. This is especially true for attorney-client communications. Additionally, if the message of your email is particularly sensitive, and communicating by overnight delivery of a letter isn't possible, consult with an IT expert on the possibility of encryption.

Finally, regarding security and the risks for lawyers and email between attorney and client, you may want to read Formal Opinion 11-49 of the American Bar Association. "A lawyer sending or receiving substantive communications with a client via e-mail or other electronic means ordinarily must warn the client about the risk of sending or receiving electronic communications using a computer or other device, or e-mail account, to which a third party may gain access." The analogy used in the opinion is the need for a lawyer to "avoid speaking face-to-face with a client about sensitive matters if the conversation might be overheard."

7.2 Letters

Letters are a significant step above an email. If there is a genuine concern about whether communication with someone outside your law practice should be by email or letter, a letter is a more secure option. A letter is a formal communication under law firm letterhead. The concerns that apply to emails apply with equal force to letters. The formality of a letter may be necessary for communications with a court or administrative agency, or in some situations with a client or a colleague. As with all your writing as an attorney, a letter should have a clearly stated beginning, middle and end.

Beyond the content, the specific technical requirements for a letter relate to the introductory material, which should **(1)** correctly and respectfully state the recipient, **(2)** provide a precise and concise notice of the matter at hand and **(3)** state the reason(s) for the letter. In Chapter Four, there is a list of 12 examples for recurring exchanges with colleagues for which the correct tone ought to be set in your first sentence, expressed in less than 15 words.

First, regarding the recipient—assuming this is not an initial letter—the requirements for the heading, including sender, return address and date, are usually provided by your law firm software program for the letterhead. The recipient's address must include the recipient's name, title, organization and address. For a legal professional, that generally requires the suffix "Esquire" or "Deputy Attorney General" or "Paralegal," *etc.* For a judge, the prefix "Hon.," as well as the pertinent suffix, such as "J.S.C." or "U.S.D.J.," is used. The address for a judge should also include the specific name of the court, immediately preceding the mailing address.

Second, as with an email, when stating the issue raised, the "Subject" or "Re" line can be helpful. A subject heading should be concisely presented, akin to the headline of a news article, explaining the story that follows. Imagine you are writing a letter to one of your more important clients, advising on her upcoming deposition. Compare, "Deposition 7-31-23," *versus* "Prep for Your Deposition on July 31, 2023: Must Review Answers to Interrogatories." Which do you think your client would find more helpful?

Third, regarding the reason for the letter to your client, the opening paragraph should present a brief overview, namely, **(1)** the posture of the lawsuit and deadline for completion of discovery, **(2)** a summary of the notice of deposition and the subjects upon which your client will be deposed and **(3)** the discovery materials you want your client to review in advance of the deposition. A sample of the initial several sentences might read as follows:

> This is a reminder of your deposition scheduled for July 31, 2023. The discovery end date is fast approaching and your deposition is key to explaining our position regarding the need for a permanent injunction. Defense counsel has served us with a Notice of Deposition and Demand for Production of Documents. Copies of both documents accompany this letter. As scheduled, I will be at your office on June 16. Please review your file carefully and retrieve the requested documents. Please forward copies of all the documents to me by May 30 and be prepared to discuss them when we meet.

At this point, your client has a clear understanding of the purpose of your letter. You should then proceed to briefly explain what has been learned to date in pre-trial discovery, including witnesses, documents and legal arguments you anticipate the defendant raising in opposition to a permanent injunction. Three to four short paragraphs (40–50 words each) should suffice. Finally, close with a brief discussion of the law. Explain why a plaintiff who has secured a temporary injunction has the advantage in litigation. The total word count should not exceed 500 words.

7.3 Memos

Prior to beginning work on a legal memorandum, or "memo," there are three things that an attorney must consider.

First, the traditional purpose of a memo is not to advocate a position, but rather to bring understanding to a legal matter, and explain how best to work toward a solution.

Second, there is a critically important difference in the recipient of a memo. It's neither the court nor your adversary, but rather someone "on your side," namely, a colleague within your firm or your client.

Third, despite the fact that a memo is not a public document, as with anything put in writing, you must be careful of what you include in a memo.

Unlike pleadings and briefs filed with the court, there are no "rules" for memos, just conventional wisdom that varies from one law firm to another. Here are my suggestions for how to structure your memo.

State the "question": In one or two sentences, 35–50 words max, state the question you've been asked to research. Ideally, you received a written request to research a particular point of law. If not, prior to beginning your research it is advisable to confirm the question. Whether requested by another attorney in your law firm, or a client, submit a short note, or an email explaining your understanding of the task you have been assigned. This is not about "CYA" but rather avoiding potential misunderstandings prior to beginning your research.

Provide your "answer" to the question: The second paragraph of your memo is comprised of one, two, or three sentences at most, 40–50 words max. As when composing a "lead," your aim here is to reduce the results of your efforts to their bare essentials. Sometimes, the answer is as simple as "Yes, or No, because..." followed by a very brief summary of your research. If there is more than one question, answer each in a similar fashion in the order in which they were presented or in the order of their priority as you understand their relative importance.

Deliver your "analysis" and explain the answer provided: This is the core of the memo, namely, your reasoning. Unless it is a complicated question or series of questions, you should discipline yourself as you compose your memo by adhering to a total word budget of 1,500–2,500 words. That amounts to six to eight double-spaced pages. That is an ample word budget to express your thoughts. Also, if you believe additional research may be required, say so. Don't wait to be asked. Much like a "mini brief," provide headings for your principal conclusions. The more simply you organize your thoughts and explain your assessment of how the law impacts the facts, the easier it will be for your colleague or client to digest your research. Brevity is always appreciated.

Pronounce your "conclusion": This section is considerably shorter than your analysis but sufficiently longer than your answer to the question. Whether here or in your analysis, briefly highlight the legal standards that influence your findings.

When an explanation of a court decision, statute or regulation is included in your analysis, utilize source notes, rather than footnotes, to provide details. You want the recipient of your memo to read your analysis and/or conclusion straight through, without the distraction of footnotes. On the final page of your memo, the source notes, together with citations, brief quotes or commentary will provide your reader with the law upon which you relied in reaching your conclusions.

State any additional questions raised by your analysis that require further research: This is your chance to shine a light on the future. It's also an opportunity to let your readers know you understand the issues arising from the original question that may need to be explored as a precautionary measure as matters evolve. Be proactive. Let your colleague or client know you are thinking "overtime" and "around the corner" about their situation.

List your citations: You must compile a list of all the legal authorities you relied upon in conducting your research and arriving at your answer and conclusion. This list may prove valuable in the future. As discussed above, consider the insertion of source notes in the text of your analysis. On the final page, you should explain those sources and quote from them as needed to explain your findings.

7.4 Proofreading, Editing and Revising Your Writing

Writing is rewriting. The first draft of any serious document that addresses all the issues touches every base, and reads well stylistically is exceedingly rare. *Writing is rewriting.*

You must make it your practice to habitually examine all your writings paragraph by paragraph, sentence by sentence and word by word. As once said by U.S. Supreme Court Justice Louis Brandeis, "There is no such thing as great writing, only great rewriting." During his time on the bench, Brandeis had a reputation for rewriting his judicial opinions as many as 20–30 times. If that seems excessive, it is not. Most capable writers will tell you that once they make their way to a suitable "working draft" that addresses all pertinent issues and contains the support needed to resolve the question raised, every draft thereafter becomes shorter and shorter. They continue to revise and rewrite until they reach a version that expresses their thoughts as best they can on all the issues, using as few words as possible.

Any serious piece of writing is best edited "cold" by vocalizing your proofreading. History tells us that the King James version of the Holy Bible, compiled in the 17th Century, was repeatedly read aloud until just the right phraseology was attained. Whether you mumble quietly or read your writing aloud to yourself, your ear will identify problems with syntax and rhythm that your eye will pass over. Despite their integral nature, proofreading and editing require a different "mindset" than that deployed in writing. Additionally, as explained by one coach on writing, "bear in mind, when you're choosing words and stringing them together, how they sound. This may seem absurd: readers read with their eyes. But in fact, they hear what they are reading far more than you realize."[2] This can be especially true of readers of a legal argument—whether briefs, memos or court opinions—where every word, sentence and paragraph is often carefully scrutinized. Reading your rough drafts aloud will enhance your syntax.

One acclaimed commentator on the craft of legal writing, Bryan A. Garner, editor-in-chief of *Black's Law Dictionary*, makes use of an analogy regarding the interaction of the two mindsets demanded of writers. He provides an apt description of what occurs as we shift gears from writer to editor. "As an editor, even of your own work, you become a critic, distancing yourself from what you have written."[3] He continues by analogizing the process of composing your working draft versus proofreading and editing. These competing mindsets are comparable to those of "the hypothetical-deductive method used in science: the scientist must call upon creativity in posing a hypothesis, then upon critical analysis to test its truth. Both elements are essential."[4]

Preliminarily, as I've told many junior attorneys and aspiring writers "Do not fall in love with your own words!" As a critic of your own writing—and of the work of others in your law practice—the most important trait is knowing what to discard. In short, as you begin to proofread your eye must be looking for every unnecessary syllable, including whole words.

What follows are seven considerations, guideposts, or "Ifs" as you begin your proofreading and editing:

1. If a three- or four-syllable word can be replaced by a one- or two-syllable word, do it.

2. If a sentence contains legal jargon, ask yourself if it is necessary and if its meaning is explained contextually; if not, replace it, or define it with as few words as necessary.

3. If particular words or phrases don't add to a sentence, get rid of them.

4. If a sentence is longer than 25–40 words, scrutinize it to see if it can be deconstructed into two sentences.

5. If you've written three consecutive sentences in the same paragraph, each of greater length than 25–30 words, rewrite the paragraph to ensure a varied length.

6. If a paragraph is over 300 words, scrutinize it to see if it can be deconstructed into two paragraphs.

7. If your rough draft lends itself to numbering or lettering terms or paragraphs, reorganize the content to ensure its form is more readily digestible by your reader.

What follows are **10 questions** you should consider asking yourself as you make your way through proofreading and editing to finalizing your work for submission to others:

1. Have you been mindful of the "reader's eye"?

2. Have you attained the correct "tone" of your overall message?

3. Do your basic points—or stated differently, your theme or your central message—emerge quickly and clearly?

4. When read aloud, does the content read naturally? Are there any portions that don't "sound right" to the ear? If so, revise them.

5. Do any of your sentences speak in the passive voice? If so, revise them to state your proposition in the active voice.

6. Do any of your sentences contain words ending in "ion"? If so, do your best to revise them to ensure the appropriate verb is used.

7. Do any of your paragraphs begin with an article such as "the, an, a"? If so, do your best to replace them with a strong noun or verb.

8. Does any single paragraph consume an entire page? If so, revise it to be a minimum of two paragraphs.

9. Have you successfully made use of bridge words and phrases to link paragraphs to ensure your thoughts flow seamlessly?

10. When relying upon citations, have you found the most suitable means by which to sew them seamlessly into your text without resorting to footnotes?

Additionally, George Orwell's take on editing demands scrutiny sentence by sentence. "A scrupulous writer, in every sentence that he writes, will ask himself at least four questions, thus: **(1)** What am I trying to say? **(2)** What words will express it? **(3)** What image or idiom will make it clearer? **(4)** Is this image fresh enough to have an effect? [5]

Finally, remember: Do not fall in love with your own words!

Part Four

LITIGATION
TOOL KIT

*The language of the law must not be foreign
to the ears of those who are to obey it.*

—Judge Learned Hand

Chapter Eight

PLEADINGS

Contents

8.3 Three Rules for Composing Certifications

  8.3.1 Certifications Must be the Words of the Witness

  8.3.2 Certifications Ought to Tell Your Story

  8.3.3 Certifications Have the Potential to be Pivotal

8.1 Ten Rules for Drafting a complaint

Court pleadings have played a major role in shaping America. A critical cornerstone of a free society is the rule of law, protecting every person's right to access the courthouse. It was in Great Britain's judiciary that a formal/civilized system for resolving disputes originated among English-speaking people. Our nation's tradition of an ever-evolving common law has enabled our courts to provide remedies in situations unaddressed by legislatures. Time and again, a single lawsuit filed by a lawyer on behalf of a client has advanced the public agenda. In hundreds of situations, a carefully conceived complaint has led to court rulings ensuring individual rights, defining the roles of government agencies, and clarifying both federal and state constitutions. In each instance, someone filed a lawsuit. That lawsuit ignited a discussion in a courtroom that then spread to the wider community. This chapter proposes 10 suggestions, a/k/a "rules," that you may find helpful as you draft pleadings for filing with a court.

8.1.1 Master the Facts and Applicable Law

Filing a lawsuit is a commitment. It's a commitment to your client, to the court system and to your professional integrity. Over the years, I've seen many lawyers—including myself—quickly get in over their heads after filing a lawsuit for which they were ill-prepared. Don't let that happen. It's the type of embarrassment you won't soon forget.

Drafting a complaint can be compared to writing a contract. As with contracts, the preparation of a complaint begins with face-to-face meetings with your client. The initial interview is critical. Dig deep, even if it annoys your client. Ask relevant questions, investigate the pertinent facts and become oriented to your client's needs, wants and expectations. You need to learn all you can regarding the "who, what, when, where, why and how" of your client's claims. Who are potential witnesses, whether pro or con? Are there any helpful (or damaging) photos or exhibits? Is your client committed to the potentially long haul of litigation? In addition to the client's testimony, you need to assess the type of witness he will make in a courtroom. Focus on overall conduct, personal bearing and delivery. Additionally, there is no substitute for a detailed review of documents, photographs or video/audio tapes that provide evidence upon which a court ruling may rest. Depending on your knowledge of the applicable law—whether at the outset or upon research following your initial discussions—it is critical you advise your client of the factual and legal hurdles that must be overcome in order to succeed. Failure to do so is malpractice.

Managing your client's expectations can be challenging. In your initial interview with your prospective client, you need to learn more than just the facts, principal players, potential witnesses and chronology of events relevant to the potential litigation. You need to learn the client's expectations. **(1)** What does the client hope to achieve from filing a lawsuit? **(2)** What is the outcome your client expects? **(3)** Is she looking for a big payday, fighting for principle or seeking revenge? **(4)** Does your client understand that regardless of how worthy the claim is, there will be stiff resistance by the defense, and he must contend with burdensome pre-trial discovery? Your retainer letter should address these issues.

8.1.2 Write as Though a Motion to Dismiss Awaits You

Begin with a healthy respect for defense counsel. They will not lie down for you. File every complaint assuming there will be stiff resistance. Three things are more likely than not: **(1)** The defense will be administered by an insurance carrier. **(2)** Your adversary will have some degree of expertise on your type of claim. **(3)** Your adversary will have substantial resources and deploy them with skill and savvy timing, sometimes with an eye towards frustrating you as well as your efforts. Start by assuming either a motion for dismissal or a motion for summary judgment ultimately awaits you.

Insurance companies have few qualms about paying lawyers. They rely upon their ability to wear down plaintiffs. Many insurance carriers have in-house defense attorneys on their payroll or utilize attorneys with law firms who are committed solely to a single carrier. It is likely your complaint will not be all that novel to defense counsel. It's even more likely you will be burdened from the outset with discovery requests with the aim of building a record in support of a dispositive motion. That's what defense lawyers do. As you draft your complaint, view both your facts and the law with a healthy degree of skepticism. Scrutinize all the information provided by your client and examine the relevant law from your adversary's perspective. Then, while thinking critically about the plaintiff's claim, draft your complaint highlighting those facts that will be the cornerstones of your brief in opposition to the defendant's dispositive motion(s).

In drafting your complaint, be mindful of the difference between "notice pleading," which is the far more common and routine form of making allegations, and "fact-specific pleading."

Notice pleading has existed under the Federal Rules of Civil Procedure and most state jurisdictions for over 70 years. Typical of this approach is New Jersey, which requires a complaint to "...contain a statement of facts on which the claim is based, showing that the pleader is entitled to relief, and a demand for judgment for the relief to which the pleader claims entitlement."[1] This type of pleading requires only a general description of the allegations underlying the claim and an explanation of the cause of action. The purpose is to give "notice" of the relevant factual and legal issues and the parties affected, in order to "fairly apprise the adverse party of the claims and issues raised."[2] An example is the common law tort of negligence.

Your complaint should contain a brief statement of the background facts, including the principal players, together with the assertion of a duty of care that was violated. The structure permitted by most court rules is uncomplicated and forgiving, without the need to show detailed facts. It makes few demands. Yet the facts recited are vital because they must lie within the boundaries of existing law.

Fact-specific pleading requires a more detailed description of the facts—or "particulars of the wrong"— supporting the claim. Though few jurisdictions require such pleading generally, the need for heightened fact pleading is typically dictated by the cause of action being asserted. The court rules of New Jersey and the federal courts are quite similar regarding "Fraud; Mistake; Condition of Mind" as matters in which the "particulars of the wrong"[3] must be stated.[4] More than giving notice, your pleading must be sufficiently detailed with probative factual evidence in the allegations to sustain a facially valid claim. An action for fraud is a primary example of fact-specific pleading. An illustration of the standard is: "The basic elements of legal fraud are a knowing falsehood or misrepresentation made with the intention that the other person relies thereon and that person's reliance and consequent damage."[5] When alleging fraud, failure to satisfy this requirement risks dismissal. Although amendments to your pleadings are permitted, you must be prepared to plead with specificity.

8.1.3 Every Complaint Needs an Introduction

At the outset, you must briefly tell the court and your adversary the *what* and the *how* of the circumstances that led to the filing of the complaint and the *relief* that your client is seeking. Chapter Three addressed the importance of your "lead." You must rely upon the same mindset in writing your introduction. Craft two or three short paragraphs (250–300 words max), distilling the plaintiff's claim to its essence. The aim of an introductory statement is to establish the framework for the factual allegations and legal claims that follow. The more directly and matter-of-factly you express yourself, free of hyperbole or scolding the defendant, the better. You are seeking to engage your reader with a short story explaining why the plaintiff is entitled to relief for the wrongs of the defendant.

Whether it be defense counsel, the judge assigned to your lawsuit, or the insurance executive overseeing your litigation, you want the takeaway to be that the plaintiff's complaint has merit. You want your adversary and the insurance executive to have a tinge of worry, and for the judge to be favorably impressed by what reads like a claim entitled to relief. Paint with a broad brush and use key facts and terms that will appear later in your allegations. Your aim is to impress upon the reader that you have thought things through, have a firm grasp of the facts and law, and are clear-eyed about the relief attainable on behalf of your client.

8.1.4 Make Your Allegations Easily Understood

In some complaints the allegations of plaintiff's counsel are written as generalities, because counsel wants to keep the defense guessing, forcing them to work for every bit of relevant information. This is not a wise strategy. *First*, there's nothing to "hide" because nothing can be hidden. *Second*, while defense counsel is laboring to learn the relevant facts, plaintiff's counsel is laboring to respond to discovery requests. *Third*, more likely than not, all the while (particularly in contingent fee matters), defense counsel is being paid for their time; plaintiff's counsel is not. By being specific in your allegations you are sending the message that you have done your homework, are knowledgeable of the facts, and are confident in the plaintiff's claim.

With regard to having done your homework in preparation for filing a lawsuit, you should take whatever time you need. Unless a statute of limitations is looming, or you are seeking emergent injunctive relief for which there is urgency, go slow. Meet with your client and take extensive notes. Meet with your client again, and request that she bring her primary witness(es) along so you can interview them as well. Research the law. Prepare a rough draft of the complaint. Meet with your client again to review the allegations of the draft complaint. If a certification(s) is warranted, prepare one. At your final prep meeting, confirm not only your client's endorsement of the allegations but also the willingness to proceed with the journey known as "litigation." There can be no hesitancy to proceed by you or your client.

8.1.5 Details Matter

Conceal nothing nor gloss over any relevant facts when reciting the pertinent details supporting your allegations. You have nothing to hide. Every relevant detail, including any negative facts that might undermine your claim, should be raised and addressed. Your allegations should present an easily understood chronology of events, combined with why the defendant's conduct violated a norm or standard of the law, and how that conduct harmed your client. Taking a cue from your introductory statement, your allegations should tell a story. Express yourself, free of exaggerating any of the facts or condemning the defendant's conduct. You are seeking to engage your reader with a short story explaining why the plaintiff is entitled to relief for the wrongful conduct of the defendant. Though, under the law, nothing said in a pleading can be libelous, avoid alleging anything that is defamatory. Present your allegations with all the supportive materials available. I've read complaints where counsel has included verbatim quotes of the defendant, supported by an affidavit, or something damaging the plaintiff has in his possession and is evidence confirming the allegation is valid. Be resourceful. Work with your client to nail down the proofs in advance of filing your complaint.

8.1.6 Complaints Should be Comprised of Short Sentences and Paragraphs

There is a distinction between providing all the meaningful facts and overwhelming your reader with a deluge of words. That deluge is frequently comprised of unnecessary repetition. When editing your pleadings strive to eliminate verbosity. You want your pleadings to read fluently, one thought flowing into another, each building block constructing the story upon which your complaint rests.

Your allegations should be written in simple unadorned prose. Each numbered paragraph should contain two to three simple declaratory statements. All your allegations, short of those that pronounce the defendant's liability, should be incontestable (i.e., not necessarily beyond dispute or challenge, but rather that all the statements contained in your complaint must be free of exaggeration, speculation or conjecture). Your syntax is critical. You will be living with your words for the duration of the lawsuit. In presenting the "who, what, when, where, why and how" of the plaintiff's claim, present all the facts you are certain will stand up to scrutiny, whether in a deposition, cross-examination at trial or on a dispositive motion. The simpler the structure of the sentences and paragraphs of your complaint, the more credible your allegations will read.

8.1.7 Go Lightly on the Modifiers

As stated in the preceding section, you should strive to craft allegations that are "incontestable." That's only possible when you compose objective statements of fact detailing the defendant's actions, as opposed to subjective declarations condemning the defendant's conduct. Don't embroider your allegations with overstatement or denunciation. There is a distinction between detailing the facts and embellishing them with assertions that cannot be proven. Subjective assertions on the thought processes, opinions or behavior of the defendant are irrelevant. Sometimes the plaintiff's passion is contagious. Don't permit hyped-up language to distract from a cogent story.

8.1.8 Introduce Allegations with Headlines

Generally speaking, don't force the reader's eye to proceed through your complaint one numbered paragraph after another.

That works well for uncomplicated matters such as debt collection, automobile injury, or slip and fall litigation. But the more complex the issues raised by your complaint, the greater the need to separate the allegations by subject matter and cause of action. To do that, create headlines alerting the reader to what is coming next. To introduce each new subject area of your complaint, use a heading, similar to what you might find in a news article. Yet unlike a news article, your complaint's headlines are designed to advocate. To the extent a new subject area of your complaint relies upon previously stated facts, the initial paragraph of the new/separate causes of action should include language similar to, "This count of Plaintiff's complaint repeats and incorporates the allegations set forth in preceding paragraphs as if the same were set forth herein at length."

For each cause of action use a headline that summarizes the allegations and legal claims that follow. For example, in a workplace discrimination/sexual harassment lawsuit, you might compose the following three headlines. **(1)** With promises of a promotion, Defendant hired Plaintiff for a position for which they both knew that she was under-qualified. **(2)** Shortly after hiring Plaintiff, Defendant texted her, asking Plaintiff to meet for lunch, off-premises; Plaintiff declined. That same day Defendant followed Plaintiff to her car, urging her to join him at a nearby tavern; she declined. **(3)** One week later, Defendant emailed Plaintiff, charging poor performance and advising that she was terminated. You get the idea. Such headlines do several things: *First*, they help the reader to visualize the plaintiff's relationship with the defendant, resulting in her claim against him. *Second*, headings make it easier for the reader to understand the building blocks of the plaintiff's claim. *Third*, headings help tell the plaintiff's story. By delivering meaningful chunks of information in an uncomplicated manner, you are both simplifying and reinforcing your message.

8.1.9 Your Prayer for Relief Matters

Be direct in stating the relief you are seeking. Whether you are seeking money damages, injunctive relief or a declaratory judgment, the court and your adversary need to know. A clear statement of the endgame you are pursuing assists both the court and your adversary in better understanding your claim. Depending upon what you learn during pre-trial discovery, you may need to amend your prayer for relief. Be certain to make your request to amend your pleadings in a timely fashion, namely, within a reasonable time following completion of discovery and prior to your trial date. (Note: Some jurisdictions, including New Jersey, permit pleading amendments at trial, to conform to the proofs.)

8.1.10 Attach Relevant Documents

Every complaint tells a story all its own. Yet sometimes, the allegations of your complaint aren't as persuasive as a document in which either party has made a critical statement. Occasionally, a single piece of paper can amplify your assertions better than anything else. Other times, a document itself is pivotal to the dispute (e.g., a forged deed, an unsigned contract or a memorandum providing the history of a critical aspect of the dispute). Jurisdictions vary regarding what can be attached to a pleading but, when permissible, attaching a single document can make your story come alive.

8.2 Five Rules for Preparing Responsive Pleadings

8.2.1 Answers Need an Introduction

There are no rules prohibiting an introduction for an answer. Yet, the benefit of an introduction is that you can tell the defendant's side of the story. By creating two or three short paragraphs (200–250 words max), presenting the defendant's position, you will set yourself apart. Introductions in complaints are fairly common, but not so with answers. Judges and their law clerks do read your pleadings. By providing the defendant's story of how the litigation arose, you have the opportunity to create a framework for the factual denials and defenses that follow in your responsive pleadings. Again, the more matter-of-factly you express yourself—free of demeaning or negative vocabulary—the better. You want to engage the judge and/or her law clerk, as well as plaintiff's counsel, and possibly the plaintiff. Compose a short story explaining why the defendant's conduct was appropriate under the law and why the plaintiff is not entitled to relief. Wise defense counsel sends that message early.

8.2.2 Your Answer Can Create a Storyline for the Defendant

Most court rules, like New Jersey's and the Federal Rules, require: "An answer shall state in short and plain terms the pleader's defenses to each claim asserted and shall admit or deny the allegations upon which the adversary relies."[6] Most defense counsel prefer a minimalist approach, simply denying the plaintiff's charges. Yet there are potential benefits from providing more than mere denials. Depending upon the complexity of the litigation and the detail of the plaintiff's pleadings, you may want to include counter statements of fact in addition to your denials. Be creative without resorting to generalities. Following an introduction and a counter-statement of facts, consider including brief numbered or lettered paragraphs comprised of one or two sentences each. Then establish the defendant's timeline or actions of the parties and a chronology of relevant key facts (e.g., defects in the plaintiff's factual scenario or legal position). When the plaintiff's pleadings have a flaw worth exploiting, shine a light on it.

8.2.3 Concede What You Must

There is nothing to be gained by denying an allegation you know the plaintiff can prove with little difficulty. You are an officer of the court. Don't play games by asserting denials you know are simply obstructing the inevitable as the proofs unfold. No matter how uncomfortable or potentially damaging, concede bad facts. Remove them from contention and then work toward countering them or diminishing their importance. The court, your adversary, and, in the long run your client, will respect your decision.

8.2.4 Contest What You Will with Facts

Though unaddressed in New Jersey and federal court rules, nothing prevents you from crafting responsive pleadings that go beyond simply "Denied." You can counter the plaintiff's facts with facts provided to you by the defendant. Often you and your client know a lawsuit is on the way. Your client may have reliable business records, notes/recordings of conversations, and possibly a diary or other trustworthy means of confirmation. When your client has provided you with credible information regarding the circumstances that gave rise to the litigation, and they are of value to the defense, make use of them where appropriate. For example (see 8.1.8), you might respond, "Denied. Defendant never followed Plaintiff to her car at any time. Defendant's surveillance videos will confirm that Plaintiff and Defendant were never together in the business parking lot." Unless your strategy for the defense doesn't permit it, when you have reliable counter facts, consider utilizing them in your responsive pleadings.

8.2.5 Promptly Serve Discovery Requests

Assuming you have met with your client prior to the filing of your responsive pleadings, and he has provided you with all information under his control relevant to the defense, then get moving on discovery.

Thought should always be given to preparing your initial discovery requests promptly. You should serve them at the time you file your answer. Why? "Facts don't look any better as they get older. Nor do people's memories get any better over time."[7] Gather all available information and then begin planning your strategy for interrogatories, production of documents, requests for admissions and depositions. Press the plaintiff. Get the process moving.

8.3 Three Rules for Composing Certifications

8.3.1 Certifications Must be the Words of the Witness

A "certification in lieu of oath" is confirmation of facts attested to by the witness (or affiant). Certifications are essentially testimonial evidence in written form. As with your complaint or answer, a certification will have the caption of your litigation and should include a brief description of the litigation in which it is being presented. Ordinarily, a certification is: **(1)** organized in numbered paragraphs, **(2)** written in the first person and **(3)** sworn to by someone with first-hand knowledge, namely, a witness with authority to certify. Those several items should be detailed in the second paragraph, following a brief discussion of the litigation itself. The affiant is generally confirming one and/ or two things: **(a)** the truth of the statements contained in the affidavit and **(b)** the accuracy or authenticity of facts or documents. It's critical the statements contained in a certification be those of the affiant herself.

There are occasions I recall with a smile when I observed the testimony of a witness stumbling over facts in his certification. When questioned about his recollections of its content and asked, "Why the difficulty?" The reply was along the lines, "The lawyer prepared it, and told me to sign it because it was needed for the lawsuit." Don't permit that to happen to you.

8.3.2 Certifications Ought to Tell Your Story

Your client or a witness cease to be a passive actor when she swears under oath to a certification. Having experienced the events recounted, the affiant is the keeper of the facts supporting the story you wish to tell. The account of the story of whatever occurred begins and ends with the client or witness. This impacts how a certification should be prepared. Frequently, lawyers draft a certification based on what the witness tells them but do little more than paraphrase. A better practice is to interview the witness and save their statements using a recording device. Then quote the witness extensively, threading it together with the overarching storyline of your complaint or answer.

When dealing with your client or a cooperative witness, you might also request that, in the quiet of home, sitting before a keyboard or with a pen and paper, the witness compose a statement recounting his best recollection of the facts. Remind the witness you are working toward a statement that will be scrutinized in the legal proceedings. If any certification is false, it is akin to perjury, for which there are serious penalties. You can suggest pertinent issues to be addressed, but the words must be those of the witness. Once the witness has completed the draft, edit the draft certification for both form and content. If the statement alludes to documents relevant to the storyline, ask the witness to produce them; you may need to attach them to the certification. In editing the draft certification be mindful of how it contributes to the story of the litigation. Finally, witnesses must be encouraged to speak for themselves. Don't inject yourself into their stories.

8.3.3 Certifications Have the Potential to be Pivotal

At the risk of sounding dramatic, there may be occasions in your law practice when a certification can play a key role in significantly altering the flow of events in litigation. It might be early on, with the launching of your lawsuit, or as things initially unfold and you need to lay out boundaries. Or it might be much later in the litigation as the record of events builds, creating a factual scenario positioning things to be successfully brought to a conclusion.

The impact of a single well-crafted certification can strike the opposition like a punch in the face. I've seen a broad range of pivotal witnesses first emerge in court proceedings by means of a devastatingly decisive certification, much like an axe splitting a log. Things are never the same. Once the statements of the witness are on the record, the landscape of the litigation is reshaped. It could be anyone from a scientific researcher, engineer, architect, to a nurse, police officer or building contractor.

Occasionally, a new critical witness emerges who can make all the difference. The submission of such a certification can be the hinge on which the proceedings swing in a new direction.

When the opportunity arises or the facts require, such certification must be created with the utmost care. At times, when you swing for the fences and strike out, it's game over. So, you must be particularly diligent. You must work closely with the witness, assembling all relevant documents, records and exhibits to accompany the certification. A well-crafted certification can be a game-changer. Don't underestimate its value, or the effort required to capture the court's attention.

Chapter Nine

THOUGHTS ON WRITING BRIEFS

Throughout my career, most briefs I've read contained too many words and too few sentences. As with all crafts, we never stop learning and trying to improve. The 10 sections below are a combination of questions and suggestions presented in the hope of helping lawyers craft more effective briefs.

9.1 What is a Brief?

In litigation, a legal brief is a tool of persuasion. It is your primary means to convince the court to rule in your favor. When all the pieces come together, this tool of persuasion can function as the springboard leading to the decision you are seeking on behalf of your client. To be appreciated by the court, your brief must deliver a coherent, compelling, logically sequenced analysis that leads the judge to the desired decision. It must always be a clearly written explanation, persuasively crafted, for the propositions being advanced. Above all, a brief should inspire trust, credibility and confidence by the court in the soundness of your reasoning.

After reviewing the brief, you want the court to have no question about the good faith of your position. There will be times when a brief you file with the court is a major event in your law practice and, more importantly, a decisive moment in the life of your client. Yet, keep your perspective. Be mindful of the fact that while the court's decision on the issues raised in your pleadings is a crucial chapter in your client's life, it's probably just another case on the court's docket. In writing a brief, simpler is better; hyperbole, bombast or appealing to emotions gets you nowhere.

9.2 Is an Outline a Necessity?

YES, outlines are a necessity. Journeys to strange lands are more safely traveled with a map, as are new dishes more easily prepared with a recipe. No matter how simple, cryptic or crude, you must prepare an outline organizing your thoughts prior to writing. Admittedly, not everyone comes naturally to creating an outline.

If you don't regularly prepare outlines, it may take time to develop the knack. Yet as a tool of persuasion, the court expects, *nay* demands, that the submission on behalf of your client be cogent, concise and precise. Even the busiest judge will take notice of a poorly organized brief. "What you say and how you say it reflects your mental habits."[1] Whether spoken or written, your words will be no better organized than your thoughts. Let it be indelibly printed in your brain that you cannot prepare an adequate brief of any substance without an outline.

To begin, pause to review—without interruption—all relevant facts generated through the interview of your clients and witnesses, any documents provided, and the materials generated in pre-trial discovery. The more complicated the facts of your case, the more challenging the legal questions, and the more complex the issues presented, the greater the need for an outline. As discussed below (Sec. 9.5), you must focus on the "who, what, when, where, why and how" of your case and then apply the pertinent legal standards gleaned from your research. Reflect upon the issues comprising the dispute between the parties and prioritize them. With numbers for the principal arguments to be addressed, and letters for any subparts of those issues, begin your outline. Particularly when pre-trial discovery is completed, some issues take on greater or lesser importance than you may have thought at the outset of the litigation. Be prepared to edit, revise and re-organize the contents of your outline until you feel confident to begin writing your argument to the court.

Depending upon the complexity of the issues, you may not be able to prepare a final/detailed outline prior to beginning to write your brief. Sometimes outlines remain a work in progress until you arrive at the concluding portions. You may need to see how your second or third reading of a controlling decision and its progeny influences those facts you choose to highlight or don't; what rulings you cite, or don't. Persevere. Start out with broad concepts and terms. As you flesh out some of the primary matters, you will discern the details you need to address in order to tell your story. What's important is to create a basic structure. You are building a fence that encloses your thoughts on the facts and your reasoning on the law. Don't worry if your fence is missing a few posts and planks. Once you have your fence, start writing. Continue work on your fence as needed.

9.3 Simplify Your Brief with Headings & Numbers

Never permit your brief to move from one issue to another without a clear structure to guide your reader's eye. In large part, the needed breaks in your text can be created by means of bold-print formal headings and detail-oriented subparts. Much like newspaper headlines, they will guide the reader's eye to what's next.

In substantial part, these headings should follow the outline relied upon in preparing your brief. In addition to the routine headings for your brief of **(1)** Preliminary Statement, **(2)** Statement of Facts, **(3)** Legal Argument, and **(4)** Conclusion,[2] you need to simplify the delivery of your content—using headings—by dividing the document into labeled sections, guiding the reader's eye from one subject to the next.

Formatting your brief to include headings identifying when you are moving on from one subject to another enhances readability. This is particularly true of a lengthy statement of facts made necessary by voluminous pre-trial discovery. For example, boldface headings in employment litigation might read as follows: (A) Ms. Brown is Hired; (B) Ms. Brown Receives Award and is Promoted; (C) Ms. Brown Complains of Harassment; (D) Ms. Brown is Terminated. Each of the subparts might contain vital pieces of information that should be further identified/labeled. These might include: **(1)** the hiring process; **(2)** an explanation of plaintiff's award; **(3)** details of her complaint; **(4)** chronology of events leading to plaintiff's termination. Depending upon the complexity of the issues, your legal argument may also need headings guiding the reader's eye from one portion to the next. Frequently, you will need to craft headings for **(a)** the elements of the plaintiff's burden of proof, **(b)** controlling case law (individually for landmark rulings) and **(c)** why the facts of the lawsuit are consistent with the controlling court rulings. Finally, when composing your headings, strive to keep them simple, much like the title of a book, or a book chapter; five to 10 words, no more. Structuring a defendant's brief is quite similar. The format is the same and, whether the movant or respondent, the defendant has the advantage of having seen the plaintiff's take on the facts and the law through the pleadings and pre-trial discovery. The effort, process and reasoning entailed are the same.

9.4 Open with 500 Words or Less

Your preliminary statement—sometimes termed an introduction—is where you must grab the court's attention. The several opening paragraphs of your brief must be a low-key factual and legal argument, focusing on your version of the facts in light of the legal standards, without any specific references to the law. Your effort begins with your first few sentences. Those initial 50–100 words are crucial. Relying upon simple unadorned prose, you must concisely begin your argument regarding why you should prevail. Economy of language is essential. It may be helpful to think of this as your first words during oral argument before a busy judge. What is your central theme? Expressed as simply as possible, what is the central point that will enable the court to embrace your position? The distillation of the facts and creative thinking this entails requires a serious effort. The effort devoted to these first few sentences will be the source from which the remainder of your argument flows.

Open with your strengths. Failure to begin your brief with a tightly worded beginning that summarizes your arguments will reflect poorly on your knowledge of the case. The factual and legal arguments should be summarized in a *rat-a-tat-tat* series of simple declarative statements without legalese. Highlight the pivotal facts supporting the outcome you are seeking and sketch the legal issues with a broad brush. This is the moment for subtle persuasion, relying primarily upon the facts, not a deep dive into the law. You must tell the court why your client's position is consistent with what the law is, or ought to be. All this should be accomplished in 500 words or less. A longwinded, uninspiring introduction severely undermines your chances of success. Finally, upon perusing a mediocre preliminary statement, there's the risk a busy judge may decide to stop reading your brief and request her law clerk to prepare a summary of the remainder.

9.5 Bare Bone Facts

I had the good fortune to represent a daily newspaper, the *Press of Atlantic City*, during the first two decades of New Jersey's experiment in casino gambling. One of many things I learned was that journalists and lawyers have much in common. To be successful, we need to develop a rapport with ordinary citizens; get people not only to talk to us but to confide in us. Better than most lawyers, journalists are experts at drilling down into the facts and coming away with the "who, what, when, where, why and how" of any given set of circumstances. Most judges, when reading a brief or conducting a bench trial, are focused on the same bare bone concerns as are journalists. Yet, during my tenure on the bench, I read many briefs in which the lawyers' preliminary statement made me feel as though a tossed salad had been shoved in my face. Frequently, in their eagerness to make their arguments, lawyers launch right into the legal distinctions of their position without providing the factual context for the case law they have cited. For a moment, think like a journalist preparing to write a news article. *Who* are the parties? *When, where* and *how* did their quarrel leading to this lawsuit first arise. *What* does your client see as the solution? *Why* should he win?

Once you have command of the "bare bones," you have the context for your discussion of both the facts and the law. Thus, as you prepare your preliminary statement, make the answers to those six questions the bare bones upon which you begin to tell your story. This is where the theme of your brief takes shape. In addition to your discussion of the essential facts, list two or three specific points you would make if the judge granted you 90 seconds to explain why your client should prevail. Finally, tell the court why ruling in your favor will do justice. Admittedly, in some highly complex lawsuits it may be difficult to touch all those bases in a 500-word preliminary statement, but if you provide a clear factual context and explain the several points—utilizing headings—that are the foundation of your argument, you will be off to a strong start.

9.6 Concede Bad Facts

It's the rare dispute in which every fact favors one side over another. Don't permit yourself to get bogged down defending the indefensible. There will be times when your client has done something dumb, negligent or downright reckless, and you must deliver a *mea culpa* to the court on his behalf. Concede bad facts. The best way to address unhelpful facts is to explain why, in proper context, the facts are not dispositive. You can argue that no matter how ugly, those facts ought not be the final basis of the court's ruling. Then, quickly move on to your primary theme and those facts supporting your position.

9.7 Don't Argue Your Opponent's Position

You win your case by making your case, not by trashing your adversary. There will be times when it's better to ignore the other side's arguments entirely. Though you cannot ignore bad facts or case law, and must always address them, you should ignore an adversary's tangential arguments; irrelevant distractions dressed up as legal assertions. Regurgitating each of your opponent's arguments is a waste of your efforts. Focus solely on your position and where you want the court to go with its ruling. The judge isn't interested in a point-by-point counterattack on the other side's arguments. She will read your opponent's brief. The judge wants to learn about your position. Stay on message. Don't get distracted by an opponent's specious arguments.

9.8 Be Proleptic

Proleptic is a word that comes to us from the Greeks. The noun form is "prolepsis," and essentially means "to anticipate" or to foreshadow in your argument something you know your opponent is likely to argue. Prolepsis is taught to students on debating teams. It is a building block of rhetoric. The aim is to counter—get the better of—the primary objection to your argument, before your adversary gets to make it, by raising and answering it in advance. But, don't dwell on it. Address the point like flicking a gnat off a bowl of fruit. Finally, it only works best when you present one of the other side's stronger points, not a straw man created by you from unessential claims. When the opportunity presents itself, being "proleptic" will sharpen your own case and earn the respect of the court.

9.9 Use History to Provide Context

Some people believe the history of civilization is the history of the law, or the lack thereof, namely, the presence or absence of the "rule of law." When the rule of law is absent, society quickly becomes uncivilized. Even if they aren't students of history, most judges have an appreciation of history. An enormous part of what we do as lawyers deals with the past. Consider the central role of *stare decisis* in the common law.

As lawyers, we are forever looking back in time to earlier decisions and the facts supporting them. Prior rulings matter. Court decisions set the standards and the facts of each of those cases matter as well. As a consequence, most judges can be appealed to by relying upon not only the factual history of your case but the history of how the law controlling your case has evolved over the years. Sometimes the legal community venerates the jurist who wrote a particular decision. You may decide to mention that judge's name in your brief or at oral argument. Though interpretations of the past can vary, most readers are inclined to accept a well-stated historical narrative grounded in the facts. Don't hesitate to posit a larger context. In most litigation, it can be persuasively argued that the outcome will impact the greater society. When the facts permit, the public at large can be framed as an unnamed party to your litigation. Thus, part of every effective argument is placing your dispute into perspective. The story of your case will have more meaning if it is presented in the context of the law's approach to the issue in question over the years and, where possible, in the context of societal history.

9.10 Don't Save Arguments for the End

There are no killer arguments or grand slams to save as the final argument, cinching your victory. Always lead with your best arguments. When the opportunity presents itself, it's okay to throw a knock-out punch in the first round and hope the court embraces your bold approach. Then, you can spend the remainder of the brief nailing down the facts and providing the judge with ammunition to write a ruling supporting your position.

Tips from the Bench

By the Number

Be certain to number the pages of your brief. I made it a practice to hand number any briefs submitted to me without numbered pages and then at oral argument, to request counsel to discuss a subject addressed at a particular page. I waited patiently and silently while they leafed through their brief. It made for some awkward moments but the lesson learned was indelible.

Read the Rules, then Follow Them

As in New Jersey, the applicable court rules in federal court and most jurisdictions prescribe the content and format of a brief. Ordinarily, these minimally include: **(1)** the court and vicinage, **(2)** the caption of the case, **(3)** the docket number (when assigned after initial filing), **(4)** the title or description of the document, **(5)** the party on whose behalf it is submitted and **(6)** counsel of record. This may also extend to font type, margins and other details, particularly in appellate court submissions. A rule of thumb is always to check the court rules first. You want the annotated version. Then, if you still have any questions, read the annotations to the rules. If that fails, call the judge's law clerk. Generally, he should be able to steer you in the right direction.

Keep it Professional

Your overall style must be respectful to the court and to your adversary. *Ad hominem* attacks are bush league and will undermine your credibility. Emotional arguments or misrepresentations of the record are a quick turn-off. Too frequently, lawyers let out the frustration that's built up during pre-trial discovery. Occasionally, there is a residue from confrontations during depositions. Don't let that spill into your brief. Belligerent comments, personal insults and mischaracterization of the facts or an adversary's position are a drag on the court's efforts and attention. Attorneys who engage in such behavior swiftly lose credibility with the court, branding themselves as unreliable advocates.

Curb the Modifiers and the Bombast

To quote Mark Twain, "When you catch an adjective, kill it." *Ditto* as to adverbs. Your brief is not the time to show off your impressive vocabulary or grandiose style. As Strunk & White advise on qualifiers, "These are the leeches that infest the pond of prose, sucking the blood of words... When you overstate, readers will be instantly on guard, and everything that preceded your overstatement, as well as everything that follows it, will be suspect in their minds..."[3] Judges are interested in the facts at hand and the questions of law raised by the facts. When a brief was brimming with adjectives and adverbs, I knew the lawyer had either failed to edit her work and/or fallen in love with her own words.

Curb the Tangential Attacks

Yes, litigation can be hostile. Most lawsuits become a war of words. Yet as a professional, your job is to rise above vitriolic attacks, so leave the venom at home. Even when adversaries do nasty things and you feel obligated to retaliate, you must restrain yourself. Not only do tangential attacks consume valuable space, but they will also diminish your standing before judges. They may conclude you are too emotional and biased to be a credible advocate. Finally, restrain yourself from using your brief to air your grievances in an attempt to persuade the court that your adversary is misbehaving. Particularly in discovery disputes, it can be all too easy to fall into *he said, she said* back and forth, leading only to a dead end.

Curb Your Ego

Legal briefs are not about the lawyers. Your client's interests are best served by focusing solely on the facts and law of the dispute. You must not permit your aggravations with opposing counsel to color your briefs or arguments. Restrain yourself. More often than not, judges will look at these kinds of indiscretions as potential flaws in your character or legal abilities. Your focus should always be on arguing your client's case rather than sniping about your own grievances. No matter how justified your belief that your opponent has behaved poorly, airing your irritations through personal attacks on opposing counsel never gets you anywhere. It undermines your credibility with the court.

Explain Why You are Citing that Decision

Don't assume a judge will know offhand the reason you have cited a decision. Do not refer to a case without a proper citation, and use parentheticals to concisely explain the holding. Take great care to never miscite a case or misrepresent a ruling. Whether done by misguided calculation or by accident, it has the potential for serious ramifications for both your case and your standing before the court. You risk losing credibility. Keep in mind there is a difference between a losing argument and one that's flat-out untenable. Be certain not to stretch the limits of reason when pointing to another ruling to support your argument. Don't get careless by not fully reading the decision you are citing, together with its background. The case you have erroneously cited could become ammunition for the other side if it doesn't genuinely support your argument.

Sweat the Small Stuff

Readers always have the option to stop reading. Failure to express yourself in simple, unadorned prose is a sure-fire way to lose the attention of a busy judge. Thus, every word, syllable, sentence and paragraph plays a role in holding the reader's attention, starting with the first sentence and paragraph. Read over each sentence aloud and ask yourself, "Is this true?" Can

I defend every single word of it? Did I get the facts, quotes, citations, spellings and dates exactly right?

A Brief is Termed a Brief for a Reason

Judges routinely manage a docket of hundreds of cases and read dozens of briefs in the motion cycle. Get to the point! Why does what you have to say matter? Think of the time spent by each judge reading your pleadings. Whether in the trial court or at the appellate level, when the case is complex and the writing is mediocre, a judge's job can become quite challenging. Regardless of the quality of the briefs, the judge is obligated to see past poor prose, harness the facts and correctly apply the law. Keep this in mind while writing your brief. Instead of trying to raise as many legal arguments as you can imagine, put your arguments in order of their persuasiveness and exclude those that have limited merit. Piling on a slew of minor arguments will not help your chances of success; rather, you will just annoy the judge reading your brief. Finally, one useful tip for compressing the thoughts expressed in your brief comes from the film *A River Runs Through It*. A central character is a clergyman with a literary bent. He receives essays from his two sons and challenges them to make the next draft "half as long." If you want to write a compelling brief, start with your original draft, then cut it and cut it again, eliminating unnecessary words and sentences, line by line.

Some DOs and DON'Ts

DO

1. Write with short, simple declaratory sentences and brief paragraphs. They will streamline your argument and make the content easier to absorb.

2. Use simple, concrete language; it permits the judge, her clerk, and your colleagues to grasp your points effortlessly.

3. Keep arguments simple. Exaggerating the facts or hyping the law gets you nowhere.

4. Select your arguments with care. Present only your strongest winning arguments; tangential arguments serve only to distract, and sometimes annoy the court.

5. Begin each paragraph with a sentence that states the topic to follow. Stating what you consider the controlling idea helps to hold your reader's attention.

6. Think of paragraphs, not sentences as the basic unit for writing your briefs.

7. Energize your writing. Use strong nouns and action verbs as opposed to nominalizations and passive verbs.

DON'T

1. Don't get in the way of the facts or the law by overstating things. Present your arguments as matter-of-factly as possible.

2. Don't include words that demean your adversary's position, such as "frivolous," "nonsensical" or "ludicrous."

3. Whether Shakespeare, Bronte, or Hemingway, do not use literary quotes except in those limited situations when they aid in the delivery of a compelling thought.

4. Don't make inappropriate comments or diminish the decorum of the proceedings. Your tone should always be respectful to everyone.

5. Don't engage in personal attacks. They undermine your credibility.

6. Humor has no place in a brief unless it's self-deprecating and makes a point.

7. Don't use footnotes. If a thought is not important enough to be in the body of your brief, why is it necessary to add a footnote?

Chapter Ten

ORAL ARGUMENT

In the past, in-person oral arguments—on *every* type of motion—were the norm, not the exception. Things have changed, and not for the better. Forty years ago, so-called "cattle calls," where dozens of cases were scheduled for oral argument, were an opportunity for young lawyers to learn through observing senior members of the bar. Over the years, court dockets have mushroomed and the judiciary is now unable to accommodate a large number of oral arguments. That is a major loss for our profession. Oral argument by Zoom has become common. Unfortunately, that phenomenon may persist into the future.

For me, a courthouse is "a temple of justice." Though we all know that true justice and the law are rarely identical, we strive for a degree of equivalency. Lawyers and judges interacting face to face during motion hearings (and discussions later in chambers) was often an inducement for solutions. From my perch, it's in a courthouse that problems get solved, not on a digital screen akin to television. Yet, that may be where we are headed. Whether by Zoom or in person, it's likely only a small percentage of the people who will read this handbook will deliver oral arguments on a regular basis. With the exception of oral arguments on motions during a trial, which must be addressed promptly by the trial judge, only a small percentage of motions, in both state and federal courts, are granted a formal hearing with an oral argument before the court. This chapter's intended audience is the attorney who has limited experience with oral argument but needs to be equipped with an understanding of the fundamentals when the occasion arises; whether in a courtroom or on a digital screen.

10.1 Why is Oral Argument Important?

Oral argument is your opportunity to bring to life the discussion of the facts and law contained in your brief. It requires serious preparation. There is a reason the court wants to hear from you; otherwise, the judge could simply rule on the briefs submitted by counsel. Most judges will concede that when they set a date for oral argument it is because they have questions regarding how they should rule, whether on all the issues raised, or only a portion of them.

At its most basic, judges want to hear from you on the issues raised by the pleadings and briefs, and how the law applies to those facts. Structure your presentation to give them exactly that and no more. The court may be seeking to: **(1)** address lingering questions not thoroughly briefed by counsel, **(2)** narrow the issues in preparation for trial or **(3)** suggest alternate resolutions. Despite these uncertainties, what is certain is that judges grant oral arguments because they have an interest in your case. There are times in a lawyer's career when all that stands between your client and a disaster in their life is you, a single attorney making a plea to the court. A single answer to a question from the bench can make the difference between winning and losing.

10.2 It's All About Preparation

10.2.1 Master the Facts

Mastery of the facts is essential for all you do as an attorney. Prior to appearing for an oral argument, carefully review and inventory your file. Whether you call it a table of contents, catalog or punch list, organize all the discovery materials generated up to the time of your motion hearing. Leave nothing to chance. To master the relevant issues to be addressed at oral argument— to the extent necessary—you should: **(1)** review the interrogatories and answers of all parties, **(2)** examine documents produced by both sides, **(3)** scrutinize the requests for admissions to see if any facts ought to be deemed admitted and **(4)** read the deposition transcripts. Once you've completed your review, select the method that best enables you to retrieve documents that might be needed during your oral argument.

10.2.2 Master the Law

If your case involves a statute, administrative regulation or standard-making ruling, you must not only understand the applicable law but be knowledgeable about its implications in every respect. You must be well-read on all relevant case law, along with their chronology and how the decisions on your topic have evolved over the years. You also need to know the facts and holdings of each case. Be prepared to explain why those rulings support your position or do not apply to your circumstances. You should have one-paragraph summaries of those rulings available at your fingertips during oral argument. Finally, you must not only be conversant on the case law, but you must also be prepared to explain how any particular ruling cited in your or the opposition's brief might be applied to the issues before the court. As discussed in Section 10.5, you must prepare an outline or "roadmap" distilling the points of your argument to a manageable and coherent agenda.

10.3 Substance Wins Cases

Relying upon the metaphor of the artist before an easel, the paint, its colors and strokes by which it is applied to the canvas are the substance of your argument; your delivery at oral argument is the paintbrush. Once you've mastered both the facts and the law particular to your case. of your case, you are positioned to analyze, evaluate and prioritize each of your potential arguments, as well as those of your adversary. By coupling your analysis of the two opposing positions, namely juxtaposing your and your adversary's briefs, you are positioned to weigh the arguments from the court's perspective. Upon completing your analysis, it should be clear to you where your strengths and weaknesses lie, as well as those of your adversary.

As noted throughout this handbook, *you win your case by making your case.* The thrust of your oral argument is your strengths, not your adversary's weaknesses. Whether your brief has addressed one or multiple issues, you should—at least for the day—be an authority on the controlling legal standard applicable to the issues before the court. You must gear your argument to what you know to be the controlling standard. When the standard favors you, that is likely your strongest argument. That will be the argument with which you lead immediately following your introductory statement. When the controlling legal standard is contrary to the relief you are seeking, you have your work cut out for you. An unfavorable standard is all the more reason to master the facts and be prepared to explain why a contrary ruling would be unfair to your client. You must explain why the facts of your case are distinguishable from the foundational case law that is the basis for the standard you are trying to overcome or avoid its application to your situation. You are not challenging the standard but, rather, explaining why it doesn't apply to your facts.

Although there may be times when it's to your advantage to exploit your opponent's weaknesses by highlighting them early in your argument, ordinarily that's not a good strategy. Lead with your strengths. Finally, you must be prepared to address the weaknesses of your argument when requested to do so by the court. As suggested in Section 9.8, there will be occasions when you might want to be "proleptic." Keep that in mind when pondering how best to address a weakness your adversary will try to exploit.

10.4 Structuring Your Oral Argument

"An oral argument isn't a speech. In a speech, you talk and the audience listens. In an oral argument, you and your audience interact."[1] Frequently, your "audience," namely the judge, decides what you will talk about as much as or more than you do. There are three basic parts to your presentation of an oral argument: **(1)** the introduction, **(2)** the facts and **(3)** the argument with a request for relief.

Regardless of the subject of the motion or appeal you are arguing, you should memorize the first several sentences, the initial 75–100 words of your argument. By this point in your reading of this handbook, you understand the importance of your "lead." You appreciate the need to refine and compress the facts of your case to the crux of the matter. Following the entrance of your appearance and addressing the court, you need to present the distilled essence of the client's position, together with a statement on the relief being sought. Below is an example of a less than 75-word introduction summarizing the plaintiff's opposition to a motion for summary judgment in a lawsuit charging unlawful sexual stereotyping:

Plaintiffs were never fully informed of the demands of the position for which they were hired. Their supervisors emphasized the glamour of being *Borgata Babes*. What they didn't tell Plaintiffs was that *daily*, patrons would rudely comment on their physique, make explicit sexual remarks, and touch their bodies without invitation. As enforced by Defendant, the personal appearance standards created a hostile work environment, rendering Plaintiffs sex objects. A jury must hear their claims for money damages.

Following your introduction, launch directly into the facts. You will have prepared your roadmap guiding you through a careful recitation of the facts, proceeding chronologically, explaining why your client, whether the plaintiff or defendant, is the aggrieved party (e.g., the plaintiff has been treated badly, suffered harm and is entitled to damages *versus* the defendant's integrity has been impugned and its business has suffered).

Next, you will cite the decision(s) that best support your position. Select the ruling(s) you believe will establish the standard for your position, and explain why the facts of your case are comparable to those in the litigation that resulted in the controlling standard.

Additionally, you must think through your analysis of the competing arguments presented in your brief and that of your opponent. Then, "You should do more than simply prepare answers to questions you anticipate. You should actually integrate those answers into your planned argument, especially if they concern weaknesses in your case."[2] By anticipating questions you expect the court to ask, and either posing them yourself and answering them or providing a quick, knowing reply to the judge, you will reinforce the strength of your argument.

Finally, unless the court promptly moves to conclude the hearing on the oral argument, you should have prepared and memorized a very brief closing statement of 35–50 words, reiterating why your position should prevail. The end portion of your roadmap should contain key words that will prompt your closing statement.

10.5 Your Style and Delivery

10.5.1 Thoughts on Style

Stand erect, breathe naturally, talk slowly, discuss the facts in detail, then go to the law. "Style" and "delivery" are, of course, distinguishable, but it is critical to combine them because when you stand before the court to present your argument, both will impact your persuasiveness. The moment you open your mouth, style and delivery are tightly tangled together. What follows are five mini-morsels of advice about style and delivery. You may find these thoughts helpful as you think about the style of your oral argument.

Use plain English. As an attorney, speaking plain English has an even higher priority than writing it. When arguing before the court, you should always, use language that is clear, direct, plain, precise and concise. "The short sentences you wrote in your brief, should be even shorter in your oral argument."[3] Your goal is to speak in a conversational tone.

Minimize the first person. "I feel," "I think" and "I believe," are all phrases that should never leave your mouth at oral argument. At the outset, you may introduce yourself with "I am Sue Morgan" but that should be the last time you speak in the first person. Judges aren't interested in what you feel, think or believe. The use of the first person in making your oral argument is subjective, amateurish and unprofessional.

Show that you believe in your client. Judges assume you know more about your case than they do. They know that neither your brief nor oral argument affords you the opportunity to convey all you know about your client's case. Wise advocates know their delivery always needs a bit of controlled passion. Never convey an air of intellectual detachment. The argument you are making matters greatly to you. Always convey your personal commitment to your client and your belief in his position. There must be no doubt to anyone hearing your argument that you are one with your client on the relief sought.

Deliver your arguments in the present moment. When you represent John Smith, do not say "Smith contends," or "Smith asserts." Launch right into your argument. Thus, you don't say, "Smith contends that the staircase was in disrepair." Rather, say "The evidence shows that the staircase was in disrepair." Nor should you say, "Smith asserts that given the facts of his lawsuit, the case law does not apply to his claim." Rather, say "When the facts are viewed in light of the case law, Mr. Smith's position must prevail."

Introductory phrases that label what you are about to say are unnecessary distractions to anyone listening. Finally, when proceeding to a particular portion of your argument, introductory phrases are unnecessary. Don't say "I will now argue that the challenged regulation exceeds the authority granted to the agency by the legislature." Rather, say "For the reasons that follow, this regulation exceeds the authority granted to the agency by the legislature."

Listen to the judge's questions. The judge hearing your argument has an immediate problem, namely, how to resolve the issues raised by your pleadings. To decide your case, the judge must understand it. You know more about your case than the judge does. When they ask a question, judges are rarely playing head games with you. When judges ask questions, they are looking for help from you. So, listen carefully to a judge's question. Then, reply thoughtfully.

10.5.2 Thoughts on Delivery

What follows are five suggestions you may find helpful as you prepare for the "delivery" of your oral argument.

Prepare a one-page roadmap of your argument. Capable advocates always know where they are going with their message. Whether numbered, lettered or bullet-point sentences and/or paragraphs, you need a guide to assist you in staying on course during oral argument. If you have mastered both the facts and the law of your case, you will not need more than a list of keywords and phrases, or possibly a quote, from a controlling decision. Once your roadmap is complete, study it regularly in the days leading up to your court appearance. In addition to this guide, you should assemble and organize all exhibits from the discovery file that you may want to quote in your argument.

Don't read your argument. Reading is not conducive to a conversation. If you are to have any chance of engaging your judge in a productive conversation, do not "read" anything other than extracts from pivotal court rulings or quotes from the discovery file. Not only does reading from a prepared text deny you the ability to make eye contact with the judge, but it can also become a bore very quickly, and rob your presentation of any spontaneity. Reading from a prepared script undermines the flexibility needed for effective delivery. As for memorization, you might be able to keep eye contact and create the illusion of spontaneity, but that will swiftly fall apart with the first probing question. Then, your "conversation" collapses. Memorizing your entire argument or large portions is impractical. Please see the preceding paragraph which recommends a "Road Map," which should contain short paragraphs summarizing the argument, along with "a list of keywords and phrases, or possibly a quote, from a controlling decision."

Speak at a controlled speed. Talk too slowly and you are dull; talk too fast and you are hard to follow. Too slow or too fast, and you risk losing your listener. If you have a tendency toward either extreme, then you must make a concerted effort to find a middle ground that works for you. Focus on a portion of your brief, say 300–500 words, then read it aloud and record it (with today's technology, that's easy), and play it back. If you read approximately 350 words in two minutes or less, you're likely reading too fast; if you read it in two and a half minutes or more, you're likely reading it too slow. You will need to work at it until you find a happy medium. In addition to speed, be mindful of your tone of voice. To keep your audience's interest, you need to vary the speed, pitch and volume of your voice; they comprise the rhythm of your delivery. The words you select are the lyrics of your argument. Your voice furnishes the melody and the tempo of your delivery. Never underestimate the power of a confident voice.

Maintain eye contact with the judge. Eye contact aids in keeping your listener's attention. Failure to make eye contact tells the judge you lack confidence in your message. Sometimes it is helpful to practice your delivery while standing in front of a mirror. By doing so, you'll know quickly whether or not you are too dependent upon your notes when speaking. If you are continually looking down, unable to see your own eyes for more than 10–15 seconds, then you need to continue revising and refining your roadmap and practicing the delivery of your argument. Continue practicing until you can see yourself in the mirror for 25–30 seconds at a time without having to look down.

Keep your hands under control. If a podium is available, place your hands on either side and look down at your notes as needed. If there is no podium and you are standing behind a table, place your hands together in front of you at waist level, with your fingertips loosely clasped together. From time to time, you might also gently lean forward on the table to emphasize a point you are making. In addition to the speed, pitch and volume of your voice, at times discrete bodily gestures can be helpful. Your head and hands can both play a role. You might cock your head to one side, or slightly raise your chin, or gently shrug your shoulders. Your hands can be tools of emphasis, whether pointing to an exhibit, palms turned upward or one hand raised as a stop sign. Use your imagination and, again, practice any gestures in front of a mirror.

10.6 Overcoming Anxiety? Practice!

10.6.1 Anxiety is Normal

Until you've delivered an oral argument on a fair number of occasions (five to ten times), you will routinely get nervous. Even after gaining experience speaking in a courtroom, I believe some degree of nervousness is normal, even necessary. If you stop getting the jitters before making a presentation, then maybe you are no longer committed to doing your very best.

Achieving your very best at oral argument can cause anxiety, yet remember that judges are rooting for you to do your best. Most judges want your presentation to be informative and to inform the record upon which they will rely in rendering a decision. Candidly, when hearing oral arguments, I did what I could to help stumbling lawyers. My thought was that the better their performance, the better the representation provided to their clients, and the better my decision because they are making my job easier by developing a complete record. Most judges share my mindset on helping lawyers. Keep that in mind as you make your argument. Judges aren't there to hurt you. They know oral arguments can be stressful, and the higher the stakes, the greater the stress.

Yet stress can generate energy. Your aim should be to make that energy a productive force. Don't let stress slow you down. Embrace your anxiety. Know that every lawyer shares your stress every day, to varying degrees. When even the most accomplished attorneys enter a courthouse, their stress levels rise; the same is true of judges when they take the bench. As suggested in Section 10.4, memorize the first several sentences of your argument. You want to have the initial 75–100 words of your argument down cold. With your first few introductory sentences under control, and a carefully conceived roadmap for your argument in hand, you've reduced your anxiety. More often than not, by the time you deliver your introduction, your nervous energy will become a positive force in your presentation. Finally, the best tactic for reducing your anxiety is to practice your oral argument in advance of the hearing.

10.6.2 Practice!

If you have read this handbook all the way through, you know that whether written or spoken, your words are no better than your thoughts. If your thoughts aren't organized, the words that leave your mouth will be less than engaging. That won't do. Assuming you followed most of the suggestions for mastering the facts and the law, and have written a brief comprised of simple unadorned prose, then you have a brief that speaks clearly to the issues. The more effort you put into your brief, the less effort you will need to invest in preparation for oral argument. With adequate preparation, when you get on your feet the words will come.

When prepping for an oral argument, your first step is to memorize your introduction. Then with your roadmap in hand, stand before a mirror and begin by reciting your introduction. Once you've spoken to yourself several times while standing before a mirror, sit down with a tape recorder. Record your delivery. After you've done this a couple of times, then each time thereafter, practice your argument all the way through; don't stop and start over when you misfire. Know that at some point early in your argument, you'll likely be interrupted. If you make a mistake while arguing before a judge, you won't get to start over. Guided by your roadmap, regroup quickly and move on. You shouldn't hesitate to record your practice sessions. You will learn a great deal from them, all to the enhancement of your delivery. When possible, assemble a live audience of your colleagues who know little or nothing of your case, and invite their criticisms. Finally, when your day in court arrives and you are interrupted, don't panic or become annoyed. Instead, listen to the question. Then, answer the question and immediately resume your argument. Continue on your feet until you have addressed all the issues on your roadmap, or the judge advises he has heard enough.

Tips from the Bench

Assume that the judge has only a general understanding of your case.

She may have read your brief and examined the case file, been too busy to have read anything, or something between. You'll know by the judge's questions and should tailor your presentation accordingly.

Drill down on the facts.

As an attorney, I told young lawyers that given the choice between the facts or the law favoring me, I'd want the facts. The law is pliable, facts aren't. When the facts don't favor you, that's all the more reason to master them. Then, use the law to shine a telling light on them.

When you aren't talking you should be listening.

Whether a comment by the judge or your adversary, listen attentively and begin preparing to deliver a thoughtful reply that advances your argument. The basis for your reply is likely right there in your roadmap.

Start with your strongest argument and move swiftly to the key points.

An oral argument is not the occasion for a long introduction and a slow buildup. You are delivering a short story, not a novel. Within the first two to four minutes of your presentation, the judge should know the relief you want, and why you are entitled to it.

All your comments must be directed to the court.

It's a no-win, bush-league exercise to get into a heated exchange with an adversary who may be aggressively goading you. Keep your poise. Digging in the dirt with a fool will only get you dirty. Don't reply to nonsense. Let your opponent "distinguish" himself. Always direct all your comments to the judge.

Visualize success as you prepare the roadmap for your oral argument.

Over the years that I was researching my first book, I visualized myself one day making a presentation before a highly regarded speaker series at a local college. Act like successful athletes when visualizing themselves winning the big game; conjure up an image in your mind of excelling before the court. As you rehearse your presentation, visualize standing in a courtroom and interacting with the judge, smoothly handling all questions.

Passion is okay when controlled.

There is no substitute for "fire in the belly." Either you have it or you don't. Those who do will find a way to succeed. When arguing a client's case, I view intellectual detachment as a deficiency. A delivery that exudes controlled emotion is a strength.

A THUMBNAIL SKETCH FOR THE BUSY LAWYER

*We are all apprentices in a craft
where no one ever becomes a master.*

—Ernest Hemingway

If you began reading this part of the handbook first, and have no plans to read the entire contents, *welcome.*

Part Five is a digested rendition of the 10 chapters that comprise this handbook. Before diving into this thumbnail sketch, I encourage you to scrutinize the subtitles detailed in the Table of Contents. When you do, I'm reasonably confident you will find items that will help you improve your writing style. Once you've read the portions of the summaries in Part Five that interest you most, I suggest you then go to those chapters of this handbook that correspond with your selections here. You may also want to utilize the QR code before each of the ten chapters. It will be time well spent.

Chapter One—Less is More

There are five essential takeaways from this chapter. **(1)** You are a professional writer and must think like one. Clarity, in all your communications, must be your primary concern. The more effort invested in your writing, the less effort required of your reader. **(2)** Human attention is a finite resource. Your audience will always have something else to read. The fewer words used to express your thoughts, the greater the likelihood they will be **(a)** understood, **(b)** remembered and **(c)** embraced. **(3)** As a writer, you have three primary objectives and a fourth overarching concern. The first three are *precision, concision* and *economy of language.* You must strive to be precise and concise and to use as few words as appropriate for the issue. Scrutinize everything you write; needless words must be deleted. The final concern is *the reader's eye.* See Section 1.3. Just as a speaker must be sensitive to the ears of his audience, so as not to bore or confuse, writers must be mindful of how their prose will be received by their reader's eye. **(4)** Technology enables prolix prose. The ability to sit down at a computer and begin pecking away plays a large role in long-winded writing. Learning to restrain the flow of words from your head to a computer screen is critical. Outlines and word budgets are essential to limiting the length of your content. **(5)** People's attention spans are not shrinking; we are drowning in a flood of information. Seize the moment, and excel with brevity. See Section 1.5.

Chapter Two—Discarding Legalisms & Nominalizations

There are five critical concerns in this chapter. **(1)** Lawyers must always start with the mindset that they have the "burden of persuasion" on the issues at hand. Why? Because you do. Our role always entails advancing our client's goals, regardless of the type of matter. Before diving into the law, distill your facts to their essence. See Section 2.1. **(2)** There is no substitute for a firm grip on the facts. When you prepare several simple sentences (three to five, max 50–75 words) demonstrating that you have mastered the essential facts, your client's position will be enhanced. **(3)** Though legalisms play a large role in the things you read, you cannot permit them to pollute what you write. They undermine your message, much like flicking sand in the reader's eye. See Section 2.2. **(4)** Hand in hand with legalisms are nominalizations, the inclination toward "creeping nounism," the tendency to transform verbs into nouns. Nominalizations will suck the life out of your prose. The "noun plague" is for eggheads, not lawyers. See Section 2.3 for a discussion of the lethal nature of nominalizations. **(5)** Worse than legalisms and nominalizations are footnotes! There are no thoughts that need to be said in a footnote that cannot be incorporated into the primary text. See Section 2.4.

Chapter Three—Style & Organizing Your Thoughts

There are five key items regarding "style" in this chapter. **(1)** Your writing style is vitally important. Whether they agree with your message or not, you want your readers' respect. What is style? It is the skillful use of words to engage the mind of your reader. **(2)** Three traits define effective writing style: **(a)** the ability to distinguish between words and structure that enhance your message versus those that don't; **(b)** the ability to craft sentences and paragraphs that engage your reader's mind; **(c)** the ability to deploy syntax, diction and rhythm to ensure your message flows, is understood and is memorable. See Section 3.1. **(3)** Why is effective writing style important? It enhances your power to persuade in three ways: **(a)** effective style guarantees your readers won't waste time trying to figure out what you're saying; **(b)** style brings a sense of dignity to the issues at hand; **(c)** effective style ingratiates you with the reader and instills trust. **(4)** "Leads" are essential. Every meaningful communication must have one. At the outset, using as few words as possible, tell your reader the *what* and the *how* of the relevant circumstances and *where* you plan to take them. As stated by Albert Einstein, "If you can't explain it simply, you don't understand it well enough." See Section 3.2 on the steps to follow on creating a "lead." **(5)** Word budgets are essential for everything you write. After you've gathered the relevant facts, and have a firm grasp of the issues, ask yourself what's the minimum number of words required to express yourself. See Section

3.3 for a list of suggested word budgets for everything a lawyer writes. Read the suggested word budgets and challenge yourself to adhere to them.

Chapter Four—Developing Your Writing Style: Block I

Syntax is the arrangement of words and phrases to create well-formed sentences. Three rules on syntax: **(1)** Use the active voice; avoid the passive voice. **(2)** Sentences should be built like good fences, every word solidly in place, each giving strength to all the others. **(3)** Edit your writing by reading it aloud. Your ears will notice awkward phrases missed by your eyes. See Section 4.1.

Diction is the choice and use of words in speech or writing. Diction and syntax address related concerns. Syntax focuses on the order and the structure of words, while diction focuses on word choice. Why is diction important? Mark Twain said it best: "The difference between the almost right word and the right word is really a large matter. 'Tis the difference between the lightning bug and the lightning." **(1)** Always be attentive to the vocabulary in your writing, and everything you read and speak. **(2)** Diction depends on subject, purpose and audience; all three drive the words you select. See Section 4.2.

Rhythm (or "cadence") is the pattern of stresses within a line of prose; it is the flow of words within a literary work. Rhythm is formed by stressed and unstressed syllables and the length of sentences and paragraphs. Three ways to enhance your rhythm are: **(1)** Alternate the length of your sentences. Don't be afraid to use a well-contrived run-on sentence, followed by an artful short sentence of fewer than 10 words. **(2)** Reposition words and phrases: English is a flexible language. Shift words and phrases around until the parts of a sentence fall into a pleasing order. **(3)** Utilize sentence fragments. Most people frequently speak in incomplete sentences and fragments. You can too. Just be careful how you do so. See Section 4.3.

Tone & Style are critical. Clarity, lucidity and directness must be foremost in your mind as you prepare to write. Before those qualities come candor. Casual, nonchalant or less than candid statements are unacceptable from a member of the bar. (Good-natured humor is the exception.) Select words that set the tone from the first sentence, telling your reader precisely and concisely where you are headed and why. See Section 4.4, for examples.

Rule of Three & Tricolons: The "rule of three" pre-dates the written word. Nearly every story is better told by using it. The rule of three adds style to your message in three ways: **(1)** The first is rhythm. Whether termed cadence, tempo or pacing, rhythm is essential to engaging your reader. **(2)** Three appears solid and well-grounded to both our eyes and ears. I think that readers are looking for prose that glides, whether read silently or aloud. I see no reason to change anything. I'm hoping that some readers will move from this summary to the chapter I'm explaining **(3)** Three is the smallest number from which a pattern can arise. The rule of three can involve anything from a collection of three words and phrases to whole sentences. The three elements together are known as a "tricolon." If you want something to stay with your audience, put it in a sequence of three. See Section 4.5.

Linking: Your writing must give the reader the feeling of moving forward. Movement helps your reader visualize your thoughts. Linking promotes movement and is a principle of coherent composition. There are seven aspects to linking. **(1)** Movement is what distinguishes prose that is a pleasure to read versus that which is boring. **(2)** Linking takes syntax to the next level. Instead of sentences, we are addressing the structure of the entire written document: sentence to sentence, paragraph to paragraph, page to page. **(3)** With linking, we are creating a superstructure, akin to the framework of a building. Each post, beam and stud plays a role in the message you are crafting. **(4)** The connection between ideas in a sentence, paragraph or entire document depends upon the order in which they are arranged. **(5)** Readers assume what they are reading at any given moment relates to what was read earlier. The flow of your facts and arguments must progress seamlessly. **(6)** Be mindful of how you move from the final sentence of a paragraph to the first sentence of the next paragraph. Strive to include a strong, distinct word used in the last sentence of a paragraph that can be used in the first sentence of the next paragraph. **(7)** Each paragraph presents a new major point in support of your central thesis. These points are not isolated ideas but, rather, aspects of the overall thought, and are connected through linking. See Section 4.6.

Coherence or clarity of expression is created when correct diction, syntax and grammar are used. **(1)** Coherence begins with you and your reader being clear about the topic you wish to address. **(2)** Your "lead" or preliminary statement must tell your reader where you are going and why. **(3)** Strong sentences and paragraphs are critical; the words chosen to link your thoughts make all the difference in being understood. **(4)** Coherence in writing is the logical linking of words, sentences and paragraphs through the use of connecting or transition words. Transitional and connective words are essential in linking your thoughts. See Section 4.7.

Chapter Five—Developing Your Writing Style: Block II

Seven Rules for Solid Composition

(1) Know Where You are Going: What you say and how you say it reflects your mental habits. The more important the issue, complex the facts or intricate the legal standards, the more imagination, effort and time you must devote to planning your writing. See Section 5.1.1.

(2) Make Fewer Words Do More Work Through Tight Construction: When crunching your rough draft, start with the large issues. Ask yourself: **(a)** Do my words flow? **(b)** Is there an overall sense of moving forward? **(c)** Is there a feeling of continuity and coherence? **(d)** If not, do I need to move a sentence? **(e)** Have I created a linkage between paragraphs? **(f)** Have I unnecessarily digressed to reinforce a position that was already sufficiently addressed? See Section 5.1.2.

(3) Be Positive & Direct: Your sentences should assert a position, proclaim a thought or express a proposition. No matter how mundane, all your pronouncements should declare cogent thoughts. See Section 5.1.3.

(4) Be Specific: You will never get to clarity by relying upon highfalutin vocabulary. The best legal writing aims to highlight the key details in simple terms. Precise, concrete, vivid language is superior because it saves your reader from having to translate words into thought. See Section 5.1.4.

(5) Use the Active Voice; Avoid the Passive Voice: Vigor in your prose is essential. If you want your reader to keep reading, you must speak with an assertive voice. Active verbs make things happen; avoid the passive voice. See Section 5.1.5.

(6) Effective Style is Lucid and Potent: It's not the job of your reader to sort through a word salad and figure out your message. It's your responsibility to make yourself understood at all times, in all circumstances, to all readers and all listeners. Always. See Section 5.1.6.

(7) Go Lightly on Modifiers: Scrutinize your sentences as if you were cross-examining a witness. Is that adjective essential to define the subject of your sentence or just an ornament? Always ask, is that adjective or adverb necessary? See Section 5.1.7.

Misplaced Words & Phrases: A misplaced modifier is a word or phrase that is improperly separated from the word it modifies or describes. Because of the separation, sentences with this error may read/sound awkward or confusing. Misplaced modifiers can usually be corrected by moving the modifier closer to the word it modifies. See Section 5.2.1.

Dangling Participles: A participle is a verbal that functions as an adjective. Present participles end in *ing*. They are verbs that describe a continuous action(e.g., writing, talking, listening, etc.). A participle phrase is a group of words, containing a participle, that modifies the subject of a sentence. When a participle phrase "dangles" the modifier is out of place, and can confuse your reader. See Section 5.2.2.

Split Infinitives: An infinitive is the form of the verb that has *to* in front of it: *to write, to talk, to listen*. Infinitives never function in sentences as verbs but rather as adverbs, adjectives or nouns. To split an infinitive is to put a word(s) between the infinitive marker—the word *to*—and the root verb following it. An example is the *Star Trek* phrase "to boldly go." Here, the infinitive *to go* is split by the adverb *boldly*. If it *sounds* better, split your infinitives. See Section 5.2.3.

Punctuation: Used correctly, punctuation can guide your readers smoothly through your writing. Proper punctuation is critical to effective style. Multiple mistakes with punctuation, diction and syntax will undermine your credibility with the reader. For a concise discussion, see the 15 tools of punctuation in Section 5.2.3.

Chapter Six—A Primer on Drafting Contracts

Know Your Deal: Drafting contracts is part of a process aimed at solidifying a client's position as she goes forward with a new venture. Preparing a new agreement must be constructed paragraph by paragraph, with a reason for every provision. You must address everything from *Who is ...? What is...? When is...?* to *What is the consideration? What are the obligations? What are the consequences of failing to perform?* Investigate the pertinent facts; become oriented to your client's needs, wants and expectations. Assume nothing. See Section 6.1.

Contracts are Private Legislation: When you draft the terms of a contract you are establishing the standards, controls and potential penalties that will bind, guide and constrain the parties. Research the law to ensure you are attuned to any standard that may impact your client.

Clarity & Flexibility: Contracts are plans for a future full of circumstances that neither lawyer nor client can presently anticipate. The most useful language to accomplish flexibility is often general rather than particular. Use of language that increases a document's flexibility empowers the parties to later interpret the contract's provisions within the context of changed circumstances. Terms and phrases providing flexibility are limited only by a lawyer's creativity. Examples include: **(1)** in accord with industry practice; **(2)** as routinely contemplated in the business community of this locale; **(3)** within a reasonable time under all the circumstances; thru to **(7)**. See Section 6.2.

Table of Contents & Preamble: Though it appears first, the "T of C" will be the final portion of the document you prepare. Always begin a contract with a preamble. Similar to a preliminary statement of a brief, it must tell readers of the contract the *who,* the *what,* the *why* and the *how* of the world created by the parties' private legislation. See Section 6.3.

Provide for the Downside: Anticipate the breach of a contract. Consider the following: **(a)** how to resolve disputes, namely mediation, arbitration, litigation, **(b)** possible penalties, namely money damages plus prescriptive measures, and **(c)** when feasible, the ability of the non-breaching party to continue with the venture. See Section 6.4.

Define Key Terms: Definitions are essential and the language used can expand or constrain flexibility. Definitions are best left until all contract provisions are resolved. See Section 6.5.

Readability: "Readability" is a top priority. *Form* influences a reader's ability to absorb the *substance.* Three guideposts for creating a readable contract are: **(1)** Employ headings and subheadings using bold print, capital letters, plus Arabic and/or Roman numerals delineating provisions. **(2)** Avoid jargon and legalisms. Use simple words. When you cite legal standards, explain their relevance. **(3)** Use short sentences and minimal paragraphs of three to seven sentences (150–200 words) for individual provisions. See Section 6.6.

Chapter Seven—Email, Letters, Memos & Editing

Email: Email should be used warily. Here are six suggestions:

(1) Know your audience. The considerations regarding your audience are basically three: **(a)** To whom is your email written and what are you hoping to learn from them? **(b)** In addition to your primary recipient, is there anyone else interested in the message? **(c)** Is anyone being openly copied or blind copied? **(2) What is your objective and/or subject?** Email is best utilized for routine communications; stating objective facts, raising a question or furnishing a short answer. Many issues arising in your practice are best expressed by a telephone call or, when within your law firm, by a brief face-to-face conversation. Also, what is the "subject" you wish to pursue? **(3) Be mindful of your tone.** Personal conversations between lawyers are enabled by facial gestures, voice intonation and the easy exchange of thoughts supported by documents. That's not possible with email. A psychological study found people sending an email frequently overestimated a recipient's ability to identify whether an email's tone was serious or sarcastic. Try to set the tone in your initial sentence. **(4) Be mindful of the subject or "Re" line.** The subject line ought to function as the title of a book or chapter, announcing what is to follow. Upon reading the subject line, the reader should have no doubt about: **(a)** the subject, **(b)** the purpose of the email and **(c)** the need to read the email. **(5) Think through your message and proofread every email.** Be precise and concise; use simple unadorned prose. Get to the point in the opening line or paragraph. Your message must be unmistakably clear in its content, leaving nothing able to be misconstrued. **(6) Be mindful of security.** Emails are easily shared without the original sender's knowledge. See Section 7.1.

Letters: If there is a concern about whether communication with someone outside your law practice should be by email or letter, a letter is more secure. Letters should be thoughtfully conceived, planned and organized, and must always have a beginning, middle and end. See Section 7.2.

Memos: Prior to beginning work on a legal memorandum, or "memo," there are three things to consider. **(1)** The traditional purpose of a memo is not to advocate a position, but rather to bring understanding to a legal matter. **(2)** There is a critical difference in the audience of a memo. It's neither the court nor your adversary, but rather someone "on your side." **(3)** Despite the fact that a memo is not a public document, be careful about what you include in it. Read the six suggestions for how to structure your memo. Adherence to these suggestions will produce a well-structured memo. See Section 7.3.

Editing: **(1)** Writing is rewriting. Make it your practice to habitually examine all your writings paragraph by paragraph, sentence by sentence, and word by word. Editing is best done "cold," by reading aloud to yourself. Your ear will identify syntactical problems your eye will miss. **(2)** Proofreading and editing require a different "mindset" than that deployed in writing. The process of composing a written document compared to proofreading and editing is comparable to how a scientist must call upon creativity when posing a hypothesis and then proceed with critical analysis to test its truth. Both mindsets are essential. **(3)** Make use of the seven **"Ifs"** plus, the 10 **Questions** when editing your work. Finally, pose George Orwell's **four questions** to yourself when reviewing your sentences. See Section 7.4.

Chapter Eight—Pleadings

Ten Rules for Drafting a Complaint

(1) Master the facts and applicable law: Preparation of your complaint begins with a thorough interview of your client. Dig deep, even if it annoys your client. You need to learn all you can regarding the *"who, what, when, where, why and how"* of his claims. Managing the client's expectations can be challenging. In the initial interview, you need to learn: **(a)** What do they hope to achieve? **(b)** What's the outcome she expects? **(c)** Is he looking for a big payday, fighting for principle or seeking revenge? **(d)** Does your client understand that regardless of how worthy her claim is, there will be stiff resistance, including burdensome pre-trial discovery? See Section 8.1.1.

(2) Write as though a motion to dismiss awaits you: Defense counsel will not lie down for you. Scrutinize all the information provided by your client, and examine the relevant law from your adversary's perspective. Think critically about the plaintiff's claim as you draft your complaint highlighting those facts that will be the cornerstones of your brief in opposition to the defendant's dispositive motion(s). See Section 8.1.2.

(3) Every complaint needs an introduction: At the outset, you must briefly tell the court and your adversary the *what* and the *how* of the circumstances that led to the filing of the complaint and the *relief* the plaintiff is seeking. Craft two or three short paragraphs (250–300 words max), distilling the plaintiff's claim to its essence. The aim of an introductory statement is to establish the framework for the factual allegations and legal claims that follow. See Section 8.1.3.

(4) Make your allegations easily understood: Be specific in your allegations. Send the message that you have done your homework, are knowledgeable of the facts, and are confident in the plaintiff's claim. Unless a statute of limitations is looming, or you are seeking emergent injunctive relief, take your time in preparing your complaint. Be thoughtful. Go slow. Meet with your client, and take extensive notes; meet again and again, until you get it right, namely, a pleading that speaks for itself. See Section 8.1.4.

(5) Details matter: Do not gloss over any relevant facts when reciting the pertinent details supporting your allegations. Every relevant detail, including any negative facts that might undermine your claim, should be raised and addressed. Your allegations should lay out an easily understood chronology of events, combined with why the defendant's conduct violated a norm or standard of the law, and why and how that violation harmed your client. See Section 8.1.5.

(6) Complaints should be comprised of short sentences and paragraphs: Your pleadings must read fluently, one thought flowing into another, each constructing the story upon which your complaint rests. Your allegations should be simple declaratory statements, using appropriate diction, and must be "incontestable" (i.e., not necessarily beyond dispute or challenge, but rather that all the statements contained in your complaint must be free of exaggeration, speculation or conjecture). See Section 8.1.6.

(7) Go lightly on the modifiers: Don't embroider your allegations with hyperbole or denunciation. There is a distinction between detailing the facts and embellishing them with assertions that cannot be proven. See Section 8.1.7.

(8) Introduce allegations with headlines: Don't force the reader's eye to proceed through your complaint one numbered paragraph after another. Create headlines alerting the reader to what is coming next. The more complex the issues raised by your complaint, the greater the need to separate the allegations by subject matter and cause of action. See Section 8.1.8.

(9) Your prayer for relief matters: Be direct in stating the relief you are seeking. Whether you are seeking money damages, injunctive relief or a declaratory judgment, the court and your adversary need to know what you hope to achieve. A clear statement of the endgame you are pursuing is a must. See Section 8.1.9.

(10) Attach relevant documents: Every complaint tells a story all its own. Yet complaints are sometimes more difficult to read than an essential document. Frequently, one piece of paper amplifies occurrences relevant to the litigation; attach it. See Section 8.1.10.

Five Rules for Preparing Responsive Pleadings

(1) Answers need an introduction: There are no rules prohibiting an introduction for an answer. The benefit of an introduction is that you can tell the defendant's side of the story. Creating two or three short paragraphs (200–250 words max), presenting the defendant's position will set you apart. By detailing the defendant's story of how the litigation arose, you can create an alternate storyline and framework for the factual denials and defenses that follow in your responsive pleadings. See Section 8.2.1.

(2) Your answer can create a storyline for the defendant: There are potential benefits to providing a bit more than mere denials. Depending upon the complexity of the litigation and the detail, or not, of the plaintiff's pleadings, you may want to include counterstatements of facts in addition to your denials. Be creative without resorting to generalities. Section 8.2.2.

(3) Concede what you must: Don't play games by asserting denials that simply obstruct the inevitable as the proofs unfold. No matter how uncomfortable or potentially damaging, concede bad facts. Remove them from contention and then work toward diminishing their importance. Section 8.2.3.

(4) Contest what you will with facts: Nothing prevents you from crafting responsive pleadings that go beyond simply "Denied." You can counter the plaintiff's facts with facts provided to you by the defendant. When your client has provided you with valuable credible information regarding the circumstances that gave rise to the litigation, make use of it. Section 8.2.4.

(5) Promptly serve discovery requests: Thought should always be given to promptly preparing your initial discovery requests and serving them at the time you file your answer. Why? Facts don't look any better as they get older. Section 8.2.4.

Three Rules for Composing Certifications

(1) Certifications must be the words of the witness: Certifications are essentially testimonial evidence in written form. The affiant is generally confirming one and/or two things: **(a)** the truth of the statements contained in the certification and **(b)** the accuracy or authenticity of facts or documents. It's critical the statements contained in a certification be those of the affiant himself. See Section 8.3.1.

(2) Certifications ought to tell your story: Your client or witness ceases to be a passive actor when they swear under oath to a certification. The account of the story of whatever occurred begins and ends with the client or witness. When interviewing a witness, consider recording their statements. When dealing with your client or a cooperative witness, you might also request that, in the quiet of home, sitting before a keyboard, or with a pen and paper, the witness compose a statement laying out her recollection of the facts. Then quote her extensively, threading it together with the overarching storyline of your complaint or answer. See Section 8.3.2.

(3) Certifications have the potential to be pivotal: A single well-crafted certification has the potential to land like a punch in the face of your opponent. There may be occasions when a single certification can play a key role in significantly altering the flow of events in the litigation. See Section 8.3.3.

Chapter Nine—Thoughts on Writing Briefs

What is a brief? A legal brief is a "tool of persuasion." It is your primary means to convince the court to rule in your favor. To be respected, your brief must deliver a coherent, compelling, logically sequenced analysis that leads the reader to the desired conclusion. It must always be a clearly written explanation, persuasively crafted, for the propositions being advanced. Above all, a brief should inspire trust, credibility and confidence by the court in the soundness of your argument. You want the court to have no question about the good faith of your position. See Section 9.1.

Is an outline a necessity? YES! Outlines are a necessity. Journeys to strange lands are more safely traveled with a map, as are new dishes more easily prepared with a recipe. No matter how simple, cryptic or crude, you *must* prepare an outline organizing your thoughts prior to writing. See Section 9.2.

Simplify your brief with headings and numbers: Never permit your brief to move from one issue to another without a clear structure to guide your reader's eye. Needed breaks in your text can be created by bold-print formal headings and detail-oriented subparts much like newspaper headlines. These headings should follow the outline relied upon in preparing your brief. You must simplify the delivery of your content by dividing your brief into labeled chunks, guiding the reader's eye from one chunk of information to the next. See Section 9.3.

Open with 500 Words or Less: Your preliminary statement is where you must grab the court's attention. Your first few sentences are critical. The several opening paragraphs of your brief must be a low-key, factual and legal argument, focusing on your versions of the facts in light of the legal standards, without any specific references to the law. Relying upon simple declaratory statements, you must concisely begin your argument by stating why you should prevail. See Section 9.4.

Bare bone facts: Think like a journalist preparing to write a news article. *Who* are the parties? *When, where* and *how* did their quarrel leading to this lawsuit first arise. *What* does your client see as the solution? *Why* should she win? Once you have command of the "bare bones," you have the context for your discussion of both the facts and the law. In writing your preliminary statement, make the answers to those six questions where you begin to tell your story. See Section 9.5.

(6) Concede bad facts: Don't get bogged down defending the indefensible. There will be times when your client has done something dumb, negligent or downright reckless, and you must deliver a *mea culpa* to the court. Concede bad facts. The best way to address challenging facts is to explain why, in proper context, those facts are not dispositive. See Section 9.6.

(7) Don't argue the opposition's position: You win your case by making your case, not by trashing your adversary. There will be times when it's better to ignore the other side's arguments entirely. Regurgitating each of your opponent's arguments is a waste of your efforts. See Section 9.7.

(8) Be proleptic. Proleptic is a word that comes to us from the Greeks; essentially, it means "to anticipate" or to foreshadow in your argument something you know your opponent is likely to argue. The aim is to counter—get the better of—an important objection to your argument by raising and answering it in advance. It only works when you present one of the other side's stronger points, not a straw man, created by you from unessential claims. See Section 9.8.

(9) Use history to provide context: Often, you can argue that the outcome will impact the greater society. When the facts permit, the public at large can be framed as an unnamed party to your litigation. The story of your case will have more meaning if it's in the context of the law's approach to the issue in question over the years and, where possible, in the context of societal history. See Section 9.9.

(10) Don't save arguments for the end: There are no killer arguments or grand slams to save as the final argument, cinching your victory. Always lead with your best arguments. See Section 9.10.

Chapter Ten—Oral Argument

Why is oral argument important? Oral argument is your opportunity to bring to life the discussion of the facts and law contained in your brief. It requires serious preparation. There is a reason the court wants to hear from you; otherwise, the judge could simply rule on the briefs. See Section 10.1.

It's all about preparation: (a) Master the facts. Prior to appearing for ean oral argument, make a careful review of your file. Whether called a table of contents, catalog or punch list, organize, *and know*, all your discovery materials. Leave nothing to chance. **(b)** Master the law. If your case involves a statute, administrative regulation or standard-making rulings, you must not only understand them but be knowledgeable of them in every respect. You must be well read on all relevant case law, along with its chronology. See Section 10.2.

Substance wins cases: Upon mastering the facts and the law of your case, you are positioned to prioritize each of your potential arguments, as well as those of your adversary. By coupling the analysis of your arguments and your adversary's, you are positioned to weigh them from the court's perspective. Upon completing your analysis, it should be clear where your strengths and weaknesses lie; ditto regarding your adversary. The primary thrust of your oral argument must always be your strengths, not your adversary's weaknesses. See Section 10.3.

Structuring your oral argument: An oral argument isn't a speech; it's a conversation with the court. Frequently, the judge decides what you will talk about as much as you do, or more. There are three basic parts to your presentation at an oral argument: **(a)** the introduction, **(b)** the facts and **(c)** the argument with a request for relief. Memorize the first several sentences, the initial 75–100 words of your argument. See Section 10.4.

Your style and delivery: Stand erect, breathe naturally, talk slowly, discuss the facts in detail, then go to the law. **Suggestions on style: (a)** Use plain English. **(b)** Minimize the first person. **(c)** Show you believe in your client. **(d)** Deliver your arguments in the present moment. **(e)** Listen to the judge's questions. **Suggestions on delivery: (a)** Prepare a one-page roadmap. **(b)** Don't read your argument. **(c)** Speak at a controlled speed. **(d)** Maintain eye contact with the judge. **(e)** Keep your hands under control. See Section 10.5.

Overcoming your anxiety: Anxiety is normal. Even after gaining experience speaking in a courtroom, some degree of nervousness is normal, even necessary. Stress can generate positive energy. Your aim should be to make that energy a productive force. Don't let stress slow you down. Embrace your anxiety. See Section 10.6.

Practice, practice, practice: If your thoughts aren't organized, the words that leave your mouth will be less than engaging. The more effort you put into your brief, the less effort you will need to invest in preparation for oral argument. When you get on your feet, the words will come. Your first step is to memorize your introduction. Then with your roadmap in hand, stand before a mirror and begin by reciting your introduction. Once you've delivered your argument to yourself several times standing before a mirror, record your delivery. Play it back. Then start over, again and again. See Section 10.7.

BIBLIOGRAPHY

Adams, Kenneth, *A Manual of Style for Contract Drafting*, American Bar Association, Chicago, 2013

Adler, Mark, *Clarity for Lawyers, The Use of Plain English in Legal Writing*, Law Society, London, 2007

Ailes, Roger, *You Are the Message*, Doubleday Publishing, New York, 1989

Armstrong, S.V. and Terrell, T.P., *Thinking Like a Writer*, Practicing Law Institute, New York, 2003

Barzun, Jacques, *Simple and Direct*, Harper & Collins, Quill Edition, New York, 2001

Burnham, Scott, *The Contract Drafting Handbook*, The Michie Company, Charlottesville, Virginia, 1992

Caro, Robert, *Working: Researching, Interviewing, Writing*, Alfred A, Knopf, New York, 2019

Cardozo, Benjamin, *Law and Literature*, Yale University Press, New Haven, Connecticut, 1925

Child, Barbara, *Drafting Legal Documents*, West Publishing Company, St. Paul, Minnesota, 1992

Clark, Roy Peter, *Writing Tools*, Little, Brown Spark, New York, 2006

Dickerson, Reed, *Fundamentals of Legal Drafting*, Little, Brown, New York, 1965

Dworsky, Alan L., *The Little Book on Oral Argument*, Fred B. Rothman Publications, Littleton, Colorado, 1991

Evans, Harold, *Do I Make Myself Clear?* Little Brown & Company, New York, 2017

Felsenfeld, C. and Siegel, A. *Writing Contracts in Plain English*, West Publishing Company, St. Paul, Minnesota, 1981

Flesch, Rudolf, *The Art of Plain Talk*, Harper and Brothers, New York, 1946

Forsythe, Mark, *The Elements of Eloquence*, Icon Books, London, 2013

Freedman, Adam, *The Party of the First Part*, Henry Holt & Company, New York, 2007

Garner, Bryan A., *The Elements of Legal Style*, Oxford University Press, New York, 2002

Garner, Bryan A., *Legal Writing in Plain English*, University of Chicago Press, Chicago, 2011

Guberman, Ross, *Point Made*, Oxford University Press, New York, 2014

Hart, Jack, *Word Craft*, University of Chicago Press, Chicago, 2006

Hemingway, Ernest, *Hemingway on Writing*, edited by Larry Phillips, Scribner, New York, 1984

Holmes, Oliver Wendall, *The Common Law*, Little Brown, New York, 1963

Kimble, Joseph, *Lifting the Fog of Legalese*, Carolina Academic, Durham, North Carolina, 2006

Kuney, George, *The Elements of Contract Drafting*, Thompson West, St. Paul, Minnesota, 2011

Lapote, Phillip, *To Show and to Tell*, Free Press, New York, 2013

McKee, Robert, *Story*, Regan Books, Imprint of Harper Collins, New York, 1997

McPhee, John, *Draft No. 4: On the Writing Process*, Farrar, Straus & Giroux, New York, 2017

Mellinkoff, David, *The Language of the Law*, Little Brown, Boston, 1963

Orwell, George, *Politics and the English Language*, Penguin Books Ltd., London, 1945

Packer, Nancy Huddleston, *Writing Worth Reading*, Bedford Books, Boston, 1997

Peck, Girvan, *Writing Persuasive Briefs*, Little Brown, Boston, 1984

Pinker, Steven, *The Sense of Style*, Viking, Penguin Group, New York, 2014

Pressfield, Steven, *The War of Art*, Warner Books, New York, 2002

Robinson, Marlyn, *Language and the Law*, William S. Hein, Buffalo, New York, 2003

Scheiss, Wayne, *Better Legal Writing, 15 Topics for Advanced Legal Writers*, William S. Hein, Buffalo, New York, 2005

Spence, Gerry, *How to Argue and Win Every Time*, St. Martin's Press, New York, 1995

Strunk, William Jr. and White, E.B., *The Elements of Style*, MacMillan Publishing, 1959, Pearson Education Co., Needham Heights, Massachusetts, 2000

Trachtman, Joel, P., *The Tools of Argument: How the Best Lawyers Think, Argue and Win*, Create Space Independent Publishing Platform, North Charleston, South Carolina, 2013

Trimble, John, *Writing with Style*, Pearson, Upper Saddle River, New Jersey, 2011

Winokur, Jon, *Advice to Writers*, Vintage Books, New York, 1999

Wydick, Richard, *Plain English for Lawyers*, 5th Ed., Carolina Academic, Durham, North Carolina, 2005

Wincor, Richard, *Contracts in Plain English*, McGraw Hill, New York, 1976

Zinsser, William, *On Writing Well*, Harper Perennial, New York, 2016

Zinsser, William, *The Writer Who Stayed*, Paul Dry Books, Philadelphia, 2010

SOURCE NOTES

Introduction

1 Garner, Bryan, A. The Elements of Legal Style, 2nd edition, Oxford University Press, NYC, 2002, p.2

Chapter One

1 New York Times, February 4, 2021, "I Talked to the Cassandra of the Internet Age" by Charlie Warzel

2 Garner, B.A. at p.193

3 Brown vs Board of Education, 347 U.S. 483 (1954)

4 District of Columbia vs Heller, 554 U.S. 570 (2008)

5 NFL Players Association vs. NFL 874 F.3d 222 (2017)

6 Hopefully this is the only time I will send anyone to the dictionary; the two words were apt, beyond resistance.

7 Orwell, George Politics and the English Language, (1946) Penguin Books, London (2013), p.18

Chapter Two

1 President John Adams

2 Rogers was an early 20th Century cowboy comedian and social humorist with a national audience.

3 Sword, Helen, Zombie Nouns, essay in New York Times, July 23, 2012

4 Zinsser, William, On Writing Well, Harper Perennial, New York (reissued 2016) p.76

5 Barzun, Jacques, Simple & Direct, Harper Collins, New York (2001) p.23

6 District of Columbia vs. Heller, 554 U.S.570 (2008)

7 Barzun, 22

8 Ibid. p.24

9 Sword, Ibid

10 Ibid.

11 ABA Law Journal, November 18, 2015

Chapter Three

1 Blackman, R.D., Composition and Style, 20 (1931), cited by Bryan A. Garner in "The Elements of Legal Style"

2 Swift, Jonathan, "Letter to a Young Clergyman Lately Entered into Holy Orders" (1720)

3 French Philosopher, Historian and Playwriter, François-Marie d'Arouet, who used pen name, "Voltaire"

4 Hawthorne, Nathaniel, as quoted by Sherwin Nuland, "The Uncertain Art," Am. Scholar, Winter 2001, at 129

5 Forsyth, Mark, The Elements of Eloquence, Icon Books Ltd., London (2013)

6 Williams, Tennessee, "Cat on a Hot Tin Roof"

7 Zinsser, William, On Writing Well, Harper Perennial, NYC, 2016, p.18

8 Packer, Nancy Huddleston, Writing Worth Reading, Bedford Books, Boston, 1997 p. 309

9 Steven Pinker, at 27

10 Spence, Gerry, How to Argue and Win Every Time, p.100

11 Barzun, p.10

12 Ibid.

13 McPhee, John, Draft No. 4, On the Process of Writing, Farrar, Straus and Giroux, NYC, 2017 p. 49–50

14 Ibid.

15 Strunk and White, pg. 28

16 Clark, R.P. Writing Tools, p.15

Chapter Four

1 Strunk & White, p.28

2 The author read this sentence in a book review but doesn't recall the source.

3 Barzun, Jacques, Simple and Direct, Quill (Harper Collins Imprint), NYC, 1994, p.9

4 OED

5 Packer, p.304

6 Barzun, p.57

7 Ibid, p.58

8 Packer, p.228

9 Ibid.

10 Ibid.

11 Pinker, p.147

12 Packer, p.212

13 Packer, p.213

Chapter Five

1 Strunk & White p.15

2 Ibid. p.16

3 Strunk & White p.23

4 Ibid. p.91

5 Packer, p.276

6 Ibid, p.281

7 Harold Evans, p.83

8 King, Steven. On Writing: A Memoir of the Craft, Scribner, NYC, 2000.

9 Lee, Harper To Kill a Mockingbird

Chapter Six

1 See Bibliography

2 Holmes, O.W. The Common Law, Little Brown, New York, 1963, p.235

3 Child, Barbara, Drafting Legal Documents, West Publishing Co. St. Paul, Minnesota, 1992

4 Holmes, p.237

5 Restatement of Contracts, Section 312

6 Korchid vs. 7-Eleven, Inc, United States District Court, D. N.J., 2018 WL 5149643

Chapter Seven

1 Kruger, J. et al., "Egocentrism Over E-mail" Journal of Personality and Social Psychology, 89(6) (2005)

2 Zinsser, p.35

3 Garner, Bryan A., The Elements of Legal Style (Second Edition), Oxford University Press, New York, 2002, p.218

4 Ibid

5 Orwell, p.12

Chapter Eight

1 N.J. Civil Practice Rule 4:5-2

2 Pressler, Annotated Rules, comment to Rule 4:5-2

3 N.J. Civil Practice Rule 4:5-8

4 U.S. Federal Rule 9(b)

5   Pressler, comment to Rule 4:5-8

6   N.J. Civil Practice Rule 4:5-3

7   Hon. Gerald Weinstein

Chapter Nine

1   Garner, B.A., p.3

2   There will be occasions where a table of contents, table of citations and formal procedural history may be necessary. Follow the court rules.

3   Strunk & White, p.73

Chapter Ten

1   Dworsky, Alan, The Little Book on Oral Argument, Fred B. Rothman Publications, Littleton, Colorado, 1991, p.1

2   Ibid. p.12

3   Ibid. p.25–26

About the Author

Nelson Johnson is the author of the award-winning book that inspired the acclaimed HBO series of the same name, *Boardwalk Empire*. Johnson's other books on New Jersey history include *The Northside: African Americans and the Creation of Atlantic City* and *Battleground New Jersey: Vanderbilt, Hague, and Their Fight for Justice*. Most recently, Johnson authored the book recounting the worst two years in the life of legendary lawyer, Clarence Darrow, *Darrow's Nightmare: The Forgotten Story of America's Most Famous Trial Lawyer*. Prior to his retirement in 2018, as a New Jersey Superior Court Judge where he presided over more than two hundred jury trials, Johnson practiced law for over thirty years. Johnson is now a full-time author and speaker (available for in-house law firm tutelage), residing with his family in Hammonton, New Jersey.